Mary Hield

Glimpses of South America

The land of the pampas

Mary Hield

Glimpses of South America
The land of the pampas

ISBN/EAN: 9783742828705

Manufactured in Europe, USA, Canada, Australia, Japa

Cover: Foto ©Andreas Hilbeck / pixelio.de

Manufactured and distributed by brebook publishing software
(www.brebook.com)

Mary Hield

Glimpses of South America

GLIMPSES OF SOUTH AMERICA.

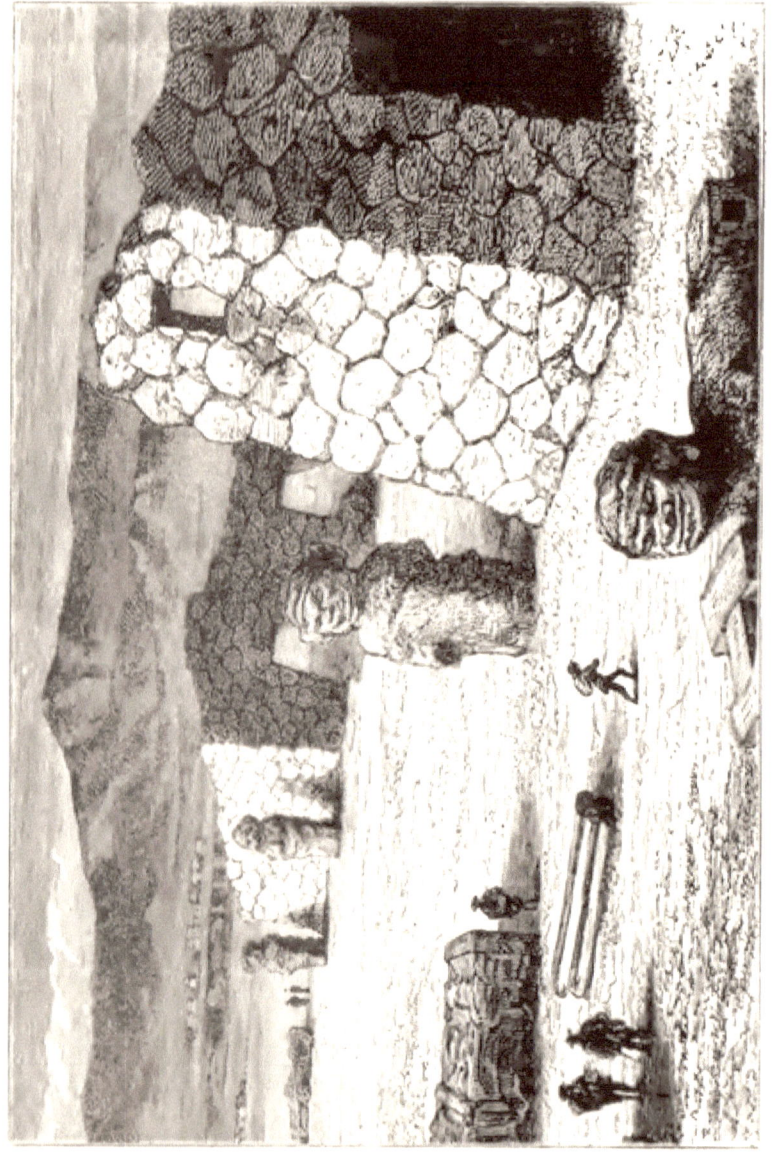

GIGANTIC RUINS AT TITICACA.

GLIMPSES OF SOUTH AMERICA;

OR,

The Land of the Pampas.

BY

MARY HIELD,

AUTHOR OF "LIVING PAGES FROM MANY AGES," ETC.

CASSELL, PETTER, GALPIN & CO.

LONDON, PARIS & NEW YORK.

1882.

CONTENTS.

GLIMPSES OF SOUTH AMERICA.

CHAPTER I.

THE DISCOVERY OF AMERICA.

OST girls and boys have heard of
Christopher Columbus, the great
navigator, who in the year 1492
set sail with three small vessels,
and not more than 120 men, on
his great voyage of discovery.

We know very little indeed
about his early life. His father, it appears,
was a wool-comber, who lived at Genoa, in
Italy; so that of this much we are sure,
Christopher was not the son of a rich man,
but lived in a humble home with his father
and mother, and perhaps many times had to sit down,
with his brothers and sisters, to a barely furnished
dinner-table.

Still, in spite of their poverty, the good people con-
trived to send their son to a school, where the little
fellow made the best use of his time, and the lessons he
enjoyed more than any others were those in astronomy
and geography. Under blue Italian skies, among lovely
scented flowers, some boys might have wished for nothing
better than to linger on there all their lives.

Not so with our hero. The little knowledge he
had gained made him thirst for more. He studied his
maps, and thought how much he should like to see for
himself some of the different countries traced on them,
and before very long he had persuaded his father to let
him go to sea.

After one of his voyages down the Mediterranean,
when his boyhood had passed, he settled for a short
time at Lisbon, and there married an Italian girl,
who, like himself, for some reason or other had left her
native land. After this, by way of earning money,
Columbus spent his time in making maps and charts,
and while thus occupied the longing he had always had
to visit unknown lands became stronger than ever.

Mustering up all his courage, he went to the King of
Portugal and asked for his help in the shape of money and
ships to go out on a voyage of discovery; but instead of
the king helping him, as he might well have done, he
not only refused to do so, but also privately sent out a
vessel to examine the route that Columbus had said he
meant to take.

In a very short time this same vessel returned, the
sailors declaring they were only too thankful to be at
home again after being exposed to so much danger, and
that the Italian stranger was mad to imagine that he
could go further than other ships had gone before.

Disappointed and grieved, poor Columbus turned his
steps to his native land, taking with him his little son

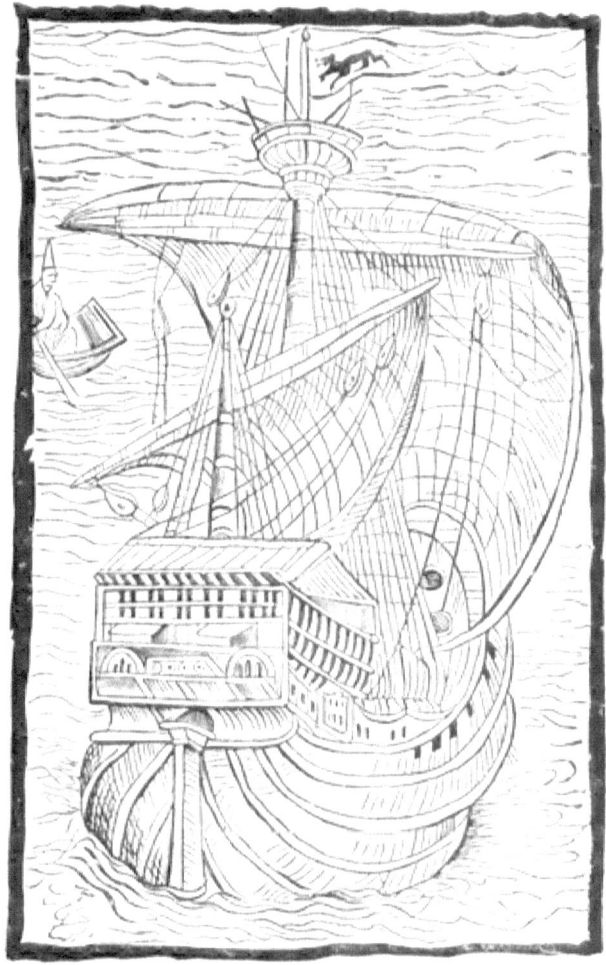

COLUMBUS'S SHIP (FROM AN OLD ENGRAVING).

Diego, whose mother had died. But even there he met
with no encouragement; his friends were all busy with

their own affairs. It seemed as if they listened with only one ear to what Columbus had to say about his search for unknown regions, and much less were they inclined to give him any of their money to help him in his wild scheme.

Still keeping a brave heart—for Columbus was not going to be turned from his purpose just because he could not get what he wanted all at once—he left Italy, and found his way to Spain.

One day, while wandering about there with his motherless boy, both of them weary and hungry, he stopped at a convent to beg a mouthful of bread. A kind-hearted priest happening to pass at the time, looked at the thin white face of the hungry boy, and then at the intelligent but sad face of the father. Kindly the good man fed the wanderers, and as they ate the food he gave them, Columbus told him what he wished to do.

"This is a clever man," thought the priest, "and I will do all I can to help him;" and so he did, for he went straight to the king and queen, and told them what he himself had heard, and asked them to help the foreign sailor. The king promised to do so; but for all that, Columbus had to wait seven more years before he really set out. It was on the 3rd of August, 1492, that he started from the South of Spain, and there on the wide ocean the brave man forgot all the troubles he had gone through in his delight at having at last gained the object of his desire. What difficulties he had to contend with, however, we shall never know. For one thing, his men grumbled and found fault with him for exposing them to so much danger; indeed, if he had listened to their entreaties, he would never have reached America, but would have turned back about midway.

Instead of that, Columbus went on as steadily as he could, considering he had to contend with the trade-winds—which, as sailors now know well, are sometimes

CHRISTOPHER COLUMBUS.

so unmerciful to vessels in the broad Atlantic—until at last he sighted land.

The piece of land he saw was one of those islands lying between North and South America, one of the Bahama islands; and as soon as he stepped on the shore he called the island San Salvador. It was not long before he discovered Cuba and Hayti, and others of the West Indies, and then he embarked again for Spain, to convey the joyful tidings to the

COLUMBUS RECEIVED BY FERDINAND AND ISABELLA.

king. On arriving, he was received with every mark
of respect by King Ferdinand and Queen Isabella, and
treated like a hero; besides which, after six months, he
was sent out again with seventeen ships instead of only
three, and with 1,500 men, this time discovering more
of the islands.

Columbus made four voyages in all. It was during
the third of these that he landed on the shore of South
America at a place called Paria.

By some means or other after this third voyage evil
reports had reached the ears of the king, who gave
orders that the brave sailor should be brought home in
chains.

Cruel as it appears to us now, that such an indignity
should be shown to so brave and true a man as Columbus, we should be still more sorry if he had deserved
the treatment; but fortunately he was innocent, for his
brave heroic spirit helped him not only to face the winds
and storms of the ocean, but also to resist evil.

He tried in vain to convince Ferdinand of his in-
nocence, but being unable to do so, he comforted himself
by thinking that after all some of his friends still clung
to him; and, instead of giving way to despair, he set out
with a clear conscience on a fourth expedition. This time
he meant to find what he felt sure existed, namely, a
passage connecting the Atlantic and the Pacific Oceans,
but as we all know there is no such passage, it is not
very astonishing that he did not succeed in discovering it.

By this time he was getting old, and instead of the
sailors who went with him doing all they could to help
him, they spent their time in searching for gold to
enrich themselves; so poor Columbus turned his face

back again. When he reached Spain, Queen Isabella
was dead, and King Ferdinand, who ought to have
paid great honour to the old navigator, treated him very
coldly; indeed, he took so little notice of him, that at
last the brave man, who had spent most of his life in
facing the many hardships of a sailor for the benefit
of future generations, was left to die in poverty.

Columbus might, if he had wished to do so, have
gathered together for himself gold and riches, but he did
not care for a life of ease. Fine clothes, fine houses,
luxury and idleness, had no attraction for him. He had
resolved to discover this new far-off land, which was so
much talked about just at that time, and he could not
rest until he had done so.

Like Moses of old, he had little more than a peep
into the land of promise, for he only went as far as the
borders of the mighty continent; other people who lived
after him have availed themselves of its wealth and
have admired its beauty, and even the name by which it
is known was given to it in honour of one who made its
acquaintance later than Columbus. It seems that when
people on all sides were talking about Columbus and his
wonderful travels, many young men and boys felt their
blood tingle with a longing to set out on a similar
errand, and among the rest was a young Italian called
Amerigo Vespucci.

He therefore set off too, and as he was very clever
and brave, he also discovered many places that before
had been unknown, and somehow or other the new
world was named after him. Considering that Columbus was first in the field, it seems rather hard that a
later discoverer's name should be immortalised, and that
the name of the real discoverer should be completely

ignored. Still, as with all of us living now the name
of Christopher Columbus will always be linked in our
memory with the discovery of America, it is not very

COLUMBUS PLACED UNDER ARREST.

likely that, as the years pass on (even when America is
no longer regarded as a new world), he will ever be forgotten.

B

In the city of Lima, which is the capital of Peru, a beautiful monument of Columbus now stands. It is a marble group, in which America is represented as a crouching Indian girl, receiving a cross, the type of Christianity, from the great discoverer, who is dressed in a loose robe. While with one hand she takes the cross, with the other she drops an arrow, the symbol of savage life, at her feet.

There is no doubt that other Europeans had visited America even before the time of Columbus, but its history—as far as our connection with it is concerned—may safely date from the day that he set foot in the land.

After his death, adventurers from all parts, hearing of the wealth that lay waiting only to be picked up in this new country, sailed away with the idea of securing as large a share of it as possible before it was too late.

Some of these wanderers were very successful, and went home again laden with gold, the sight of which filled many a heart with envy. Others settled down and made homes for themselves in the strange land, among the red men, who were the real inhabitants, and thus a great change has come over America within the last two or three hundred years.

It is not now the abode of red men only, but of people from all parts of the earth, and therefore it is that we have gained a great deal of information respecting it.

What we now propose to do is to take a peep, or rather as good a look as we can, at the south of the country to which Columbus introduced us more than three hundred years ago. The whole of the continent of America is so large that on the map our British islands looks quite small and unimportant. If, therefore, we succeed in gaining a little information about the southern half of this huge continent, we need not altogether be dissatisfied. We shall no doubt be anxious then to learn something about the northern portion.

Even the children living now know more about it than Columbus did, because so many people have, since his time, been to see it; and although it has not proved to be a perfect paradise, as some people fancied it would, it is very full of interest.

THE THREE SHIPS OF COLUMBUS.

B 2

CHAPTER II.

PERU.

WHY America should have been called the New World is rather strange, because the travellers who have visited it tell us that it must be really a very old world; for this reason, that a great many old temples and figures, and buildings of all kinds, have been dug up from beneath the earth's surface.

As it is utterly impossible that such things should have come there by chance, they prove to us that people must have existed hundreds—and perhaps thousands—of years ago, who were clever enough to make them. It is not likely we shall ever know who these people were, for they have left no written record of themselves, excepting the characters or hieroglyphics, as they are called, which are cut out on some of the huge stone blocks that have been dug up; and these characters, which no doubt mean a very great deal, are not intelligible to us.

All that we can do, therefore, is to look at the country as it is now, and to trace its history in the past as far back as ever we can. Perhaps the most simple way of doing this will be to examine its different divisions or countries one after another. There will, no doubt, be a little that is interesting to remember about each one—what the inhabitants are like, what are their occupations, how they are governed, what trees and flowers grow, what animals roam about, and many other things.

On looking at our map we find that South America is almost a triangle, and that it is divided into the following states. First of all there is the empire of Brazil, which constitutes nearly half the continent, then there are the republics of Colombia (or New Granada), Venezuela, Ecuador, Peru, Bolivia, and Chili, the Argentine Republic, Paraguay and Uruguay; besides which is the province of Guyana, belonging to England, Holland, and France, and in addition still is Patagonia, a country that is so thoroughly an independent Indian territory that it is not usually included among the other states.

Of all the divisions we have mentioned, there is perhaps not one more interesting than Peru; so, although it is not nearly equal in size to Brazil, we will do it the honour of paying to it the first of our imaginary visits.

Unfortunately, however, the more we learn about it the more we are convinced that a great deal of its history we can never know, because the first inhabitants have been dead for many ages, and as we said before,

A STORM IN THE ANDES.

have not written any books or left any definite record to tell us who they were, where they came from, and many other particulars, respecting which we should like to be enlightened.

Down the west coast of it are the lofty Andes, which are capped with snow at the summit; while below in some parts are lovely shrubs and flowers, and birds warbling their sweet notes among the thick waving branches.

Grand as these mountains are, travellers who venture to ascend their steep and rocky sides run great risk of being thrown down a deep precipice, or dashed into some deep dark chasm.

The Indian natives get accustomed to the narrow winding zigzag paths, and are almost as surefooted as the mules under their charge; but to every one else the task is much more difficult, especially if, in the midst of the ascent, a hailstorm should overtake the traveller. We who have never crossed the Andes, can form no idea of the violence of one of these storms.

The hailstones are something tremendous, coming down with such force as to stun not only the riders but also the patient mules; all that the poor traveller can do is to turn his back to the wind, and shield himself from danger by hiding his neck and ears in the folds of his cloak.

The Cordilleras are the high mountains that divide Peru and Chili from the rest of South America, and very dangerous it is for travellers to attempt to cross them, on account of the tremendous snowstorms, which come on quite suddenly.

On account of these snowstorms, houses of refuge are built among the mountains, with thick brick walls, and

A TRAVELLER'S SHELTER IN THE ANDES.

with nothing but loopholes for the windows; and even then, within these snug houses, travellers have frequently been frozen to death.

Once ten poor travellers were overtaken in one of these dreadful storms, and finding it useless to attempt proceeding further on their journey, they managed to squeeze themselves into one of the houses of refuge, which they saw standing empty.

How long they had been obliged to remain there no one ever knew, for when they were found, six of them were quite dead, and the other four were nearly so; they could not speak. Having no food, they had killed their mules and eaten them, and also their one faithful dog; the door they had pulled from its hinges, and broken into pieces to burn for firewood. All this told a sad silent tale of what the poor creatures had had to endure.

In the minds of most of us, the names of Peru and Pizarro are linked together, because it was a young Spaniard of the name of Pizarro who, soon after the death of Columbus, conquered the country and took possession of it.

Different adventurers kept returning from the newly discovered world, with wonderful tales of the quantities of gold and silver that were to be found. So Pizarro, who, as a little boy, had spent a great deal of his time doing nothing better than minding pigs, determined to change his occupation, and see for himself this fairy land, which was being so much talked about. On landing on the foreign shore, he managed to gain favour with the natives, who gave him presents of gold and silver ornaments, and silk and woollen cloths of their own manufacture, and some animals called alpacas.

These he took back to the Spanish king, as proof of what he had seen ; and as a reward, the king made him governor of Peru, and secured to him the right of the discovery of the place.

Pizarro joyfully returned to the land of gold. The people he found living there were called Incas, who were very clever, and, as Pizarro soon found out, were much wiser in many ways than he was himself ; but how long they had been there, they could not tell him. This much he ascertained, however—that they were by no means the first inhabitants of the place ; long before their time, a race of people had dwelt on the ground where they then stood, who must have been quite as advanced in civilisation, or even more so, than they were themselves. This fact has been confirmed in later years by other visitors to Peru, who have dug out ruins of buildings and idols, that had no doubt been swallowed up at some time by earthquakes.

Not very long ago, a number of idols were dug up, some of which were thirty feet long. What they proved, of course as they were taken out of the darkness, was, that at some period in that region, idolatry had prevailed. Besides which, they are specimens of what the people could do in the way of architecture. Indeed, all the old remains that were found told some tale or other. Buried prisons, for instance, told us that crimes had been punished by confinement, and cooking utensils explained to us how the food of the people used to be prepared.

According to tradition, we are told that Manco, the first Inca, and his wife Mama Oello, first made their appearance on the borders of the lake Titicaca. They said the sun was their father, and that he had sent them down to their fellow creatures to be their teachers.

Manco had in his hand a golden wand, which he said would at some particular spot disappear, when he struck the ground with it.

One day, as he and his wife were travelling, they came to the plain of Cuzco, when all at once Manco struck his golden wand. It immediately disappeared, so at Cuzco he built his capital, and afterwards was built

SCENE IN A PERUVIAN FOREST.

there the magnificent Temple of the Sun, called Cori-cancha, or Place of Gold.

From all we have heard, this temple must have been most gorgeous; almost as splendid as the sun himself, of which it was the representation.

On the western wall was fixed an immense human face, made of gold, from which golden rays darted in every direction. In other parts of the building were golden images, plates, and figures of all descriptions. So that when the real sun himself shed his glorious beams into the edifice, the place was one mass of light and splendour.

INTERIOR OF THE TEMPLE OF THE SUN.

Underneath the great face of gold were a number of golden chairs in which were seated the embalmed bodies of the old Inca rulers.

In the court outside, smaller temples were built, one to the Moon, one to Venus, one to the Pleiades, one to the Thunder and Lightning, and one to the Rainbow, all of which were richly decorated with gold and silver. At the present time a church and a convent stand on the place once occupied by the Temple of the Sun.

According to the legend, Manco, after losing his

ENTRANCE TO PIZARRO'S HOUSE AT CUZCO.

golden wand, became ruler and priest in the land; he made laws, taught the men how to dig, sow, and build, while at the same time Mama his wife taught the women to weave and spin. After thus spending their lives for forty years, they returned to the Sun their father, and were seen no more.

A great many Incas ruled after Manco, and very good industrious lives the people seem to have led. At that time Cuzco was their chief city. From it roads led to all other parts of the kingdom, and as there were no

INDIAN OF CUZCO.

steam engines then, or telegraph wires, or telephones, as there are in our days, these clever people had to invent other means of carrying on communication with each other.

INDIANS OF CUZCO.

Why the Spaniards should wish to go and disturb a
set of people who knew so well how to manage their own
affairs is certainly a matter of surprise.

Along all the most important roads, especially that

AN INCA EMPEROR.

leading from Cuzco, small buildings were erected about
five miles apart from each other. Their use may be thus
explained :—When the government officers had messages
to send to different towns, runners were employed for the
purpose. The first runner would scamper off for five miles
with the message to the first station, where he delivered it
up to a second runner, who carried it to the next station,
and so on until the whole distance was accomplished ; and
even though the course was often hilly and rugged, it was
astonishing how swiftly these men covered the ground.

As a proof of this it is said that fresh fish that had been caught one day on the coast used to be eaten the next day three hundred miles away, and that it was conveyed all this distance by the runners.

The Inca, who was both king and priest in one, was held in great reverence by his subjects, and no wonder, when both he and they quite believed that, like Manco of old, he had originally proceeded from their god the Sun. Even his most familiar courtiers were only allowed to enter his presence barefoot, and even then they always carried with them some burden as a token of the homage they wished to offer to their ruler.

The share of land owned by the Inca was carefully cultivated by his people. They would as soon have thought of neglecting to till their own land as of leaving his portion uncared for. Just the same it was with their manufactures. They first made articles for themselves, then they worked for the Inca; in fact, they seem to have been just like one great family. Instead of each person striving to make only himself rich and happy and comfortable, the aim of every individual was to work for the benefit of others.

Some great man has said that the difference that exists between "seeing that no one cheats you," "and seeing that you cheat no one," is as great as the difference between riding in a market cart and riding in a chariot. If so, these old Incas were as happy as if they rode in chariots all day long, for they were all busy in looking after and helping each other; and somehow, while doing this, their own affairs never suffered from neglect.

C

CHAPTER III.

MORE ABOUT PERU.

WHEN Pizarro landed at Peru with his few followers, this happy state of things had been going on for many years, although just at that very time a quarrel had arisen between two brothers as to which of them had the greatest claim to succeed to the throne in the place of the late Inca their father.

Pizarro, who was a daring bold man, killed Atahualpa, one of the brothers, who was just about to lay claim to the throne after having subdued his rival brother, and then marched with his men into Cuzco, at that time the capital of Peru.

What had first induced Pizarro to cross the seas at all was the prospect of the vast wealth he expected to secure for himself, so as soon as he found he was master of Cuzco, he looked about for what he could pick up in the way of gold and silver.

It is said that one soldier alone took for his share the golden image of the Sun from the temple, and all

PIZARRO.

the others took as much as they could carry. Pizarro, at last satisfied with his treasures, marched west to the banks of the River Rimac, and there built for himself what he called "The City of the Kings." The

c 2

CROSSING A BRIDGE IN PERU.

name was soon afterwards changed to Lima, and it is now the capital of Peru.

Among the soldiers who assisted Pizarro in his conquest of this province was one called Almagro, who was as eager for wealth as Pizarro himself, and who certainly succeeded in gaining a considerable amount of treasure.

Once, when Pizarro had gone to Spain to take a quantity of valuable presents to his friends, Almagro attempted to make himself master of Lima.

Pizarro was so enraged that, on his return he ordered him to be put to death, but in revenge the son of Almagro assassinated Pizarro, and thus ended the life of the conqueror of Peru.

From this period the old Incas began to sink into obscurity, Peru gradually became the property of their conquerors the Spaniards, and for many years the country was the scene of war and bloodshed.

The original natives rebelled against these Spanish invaders, as well they might ; but they resisted in vain, for the Spaniards were not only skilful warriors but were well supplied with powerful weapons, so that in course of time the whole of Peru belonged to Spain.

Cruel hard masters these Spaniards proved themselves to be, until at last, at a great battle that was fought in 1824, at Ayacucho, the Peruvians conquered their enemies, and now they are free from the Spanish yoke.

How famous Peru has always been for her gold and silver mines, even children have long known, when in one of their hymns have sung :—

> "I would not change my native land
> For rich Peru, with all her gold ;
> A nobler prize lies in my hand
> Than East or Western Indies hold."

That she should become less rich in gold and silver we none of us desire, but that all who dwell on her soil should not prefer wealth that can be handled and spent to higher and more enduring treasures, is the earnest wish of every one of us.

One town in Peru, called Pachacamac, was in ancient times a sacred city: a beautiful temple stood there, which pilgrims from distant parts used to visit, and in doing so

ANCIENT PERUVIAN IDOLS.

were allowed to pass unmolested by the different tribes on the way.

The place was a very busy scene in those days; there were a great many inhabitants; and a number of little inns, called tambos, were erected for the accommodation of the pilgrims.

Pachacamac, one modern traveller tells us, is a wonderful place. By the side of the temple, and situated on a hill, is a well built house, with fine enclosures or walls, which the Indians say is the house of the Sun. There are also in the town many other large houses, with terraces like those in Spain.

It must be a very old place, for there are numerous fallen edifices. It has been surrounded by a wall, although now most of it has fallen. It has large gates for entering, and also streets. Its principal chief is called Taurichumbi, and there are many other chiefs, though instead of being now the grand city it was formerly, it is, we are told, one mass of ruins, for it was one of the places taken and destroyed by the Spaniards at the time of their invasion.

It is, indeed, little more than a village, the houses of which are built of canes and rushes, and the most important object to be seen among the ruins is a large cemetery containing numberless graves, resting places, no doubt, of hundreds of the old Incas.

We can imagine how much wealth those old Indians gave to their temple when we are told that when it was being destroyed one of Pizarro's pilots asked if for his share of the prize he might have the nails and tacks which bore the sacred name on the walls of the temple, and on the request being granted to him he gathered together and took away thirty-two thousand ounces of treasure.

It is very little we should know about this strange place that is now in ruins, if it were not for all the graves it contains; and though dead men cannot speak, these graves tell us in silent language a great deal about the past.

The old inhabitants, it seems, never attained to a written language, but fortunately they were accustomed to bury with their dead the things they most cared for when living, and from these we find out some of their

habits, and what their religious notions and beliefs
were.

One grave, for instance, was found of a man, his wife,
and three children.

The man had evidently been a fisherman, for round
his neck was hung a net made of the twisted fibre of a
plant, and wrapped in a cloth between his feet were some
fishing lines of different sizes, and some copper hooks.
Under each arm was a roll of white alpaca wool, and in
his mouth a small thin copper coin, meant, very likely,
to pay his way across the river of death. It was the
custom of the ancient Greeks to adopt the same plan of
putting a coin into the mouths of their dead friends.

The body of the wife was wrapped in a sheet of fine
cotton cloth, on which were woven figures of the sacred
monkey. In one hand she held a comb made of fishes'
fins stuck into a slip of hard palm-tree wood. In her
other hand was part of a fan with a cane handle, and
to which were still attached the faded feathers of parrots
and humming-birds. Around her neck was a necklace
of shells that almost fell to pieces when exposed to the
air and light.

Resting between the body and bent-up knees (for in
that position most of the dead people were buried) were
several domestic articles, among them an ancient spindle
for spinning cotton, half covered with spun thread. The
Indian women of the present time use the same kind of
spindle. By her side was a prettily made bag, of coloured
cotton cloth, containing first of all some Lima beans; a
few pods of cotton; some fragments of a silver ornament; two little silver rings that most likely had been
coins; and a number of small valuable beads.

In the box containing the body of the little girl

were some pieces of knitting that the child had done; in some places the stitches were dropped, just as though the little learner had been taking her first lessons.

Then there were braids of thread of various thickness, that had evidently been kept to show how the little girl had improved in her weaving and winding as she grew older. There were also skeins of thread, strips of coloured cloth, knitted and woven pouches of all sizes, needles of bone and of bronze, a comb, a bronze knife, and a little fan. In addition to all these things, there was a little piece of polished iron that had no doubt served as a looking-glass, a netting needle of very hard wood, and a crushed gold butterfly that the little girl had most likely treasured very much.

On her arm hung a thin silver bracelet, and at her feet lay the dried body of a parrot, that had once been the child's pet, no doubt. The burial of all these articles with the dead bodies proved that the inhabitants of Pachacamac believed in a future state, and thought that the buried things would be useful to the possessors of them in another world.

The little boy had a sling tied tightly round his forehead, and then, what seems still more strange, a quantity of pans and pots were lying in the vault, the people who put them there evidently thinking that even after death their friends would require food.

If only life would but return to some of these dead people for a time, how much they could tell us that we should like to know; but of course their voices are for ever mute, and no sound will ever again reach their ears.

CHAPTER IV.

AS we have just heard, the town chosen by the great Spaniard Pizarro to be the capital of his newly-found empire was Lima. The ancient capital was Cuzco; but Pizarro, wishing to found quite a new kingdom, to take the place of that of the old Incas, said that Lima, or, as its name signifies, the City of the Kings, should henceforth be the capital of his conquered dominions.

That he should have fixed upon so unhealthy a spot is to be deplored. It is said that when the last of the Incas heard where Pizarro had decided to found his Spanish city, he was greatly rejoiced, exclaiming that soon very few of the residents would remain alive; and it is also said that, long before the arrival of the Spaniards, Lima was a spot fixed upon for the banishment of criminals, who, owing to the miserable climate, very soon died.

VIEW OF LIMA, FROM THE RIVER RIMAC.

During what is called the winter season, the fog and damp are so prevalent that for many days and weeks the sun is invisible, and although it may be true that it "never rains in Lima," the mist is often so dense that travellers need to carry umbrellas to protect themselves from it.

Not far from this old city are the ruins of a temple which must have been almost as gorgeous as that at Pachacamac.

Within it stood an idol, which, so it was said, really spoke; therefore it was called *Rimac*, a word meaning "a thing that talks," and it is really from this idol that the city takes its name, the letter R being changed into L. The priests, of course, knew well enough that the idol did not really speak, although they tried to deceive the people by saying that it did so. The fact was that one of the priests used to conceal himself in the hollow image; consequently it was very easy to deceive the poor people.

Twelve or fourteen miles from Lima are the remains of another large city called Cajamarquilla, the history of which no one knows, but which consists of groups of buildings with streets passing between them, and where men, and women, and children long ago were as busy carrying on their daily work as any of us now are. The apartments in some of the buildings are connected by narrow, dark passages, and there are curiously-shaped holes dug far down in the hard ground, meant possibly to serve as store-rooms for food.

The place may have been destroyed at some time by an earthquake, for Lima has been called the City of Earthquakes. Five or six times it has been almost destroyed by them, and very often, even now, the people, as they lie in bed at night, are awakened by a rumbling noise underground, which makes them rather fearful that one of the dreaded visitors is at hand.

They are so frightened sometimes that even at midnight the people rush out of their houses calling "Mercy!" and the priests invite them to assemble for prayers, by causing the bells to toll.

It is not improbable, therefore, that the poor creatures who lived in Cajamarquilla had to suffer one of these dreadful shocks; but as they have left no record of themselves in any way, we can only guess what their real fate has been.

After all the changes it has undergone, Lima still is a rich, gay city, containing within its walls the bones of its great founder Pizarro. As a proof of its wealth, one of its viceroys once rode through the streets, over a pavement of solid ingots of silver, on a horse whose mane was strung with pearls, and whose shoes were of gold—so much do the inhabitants think of wealth and show. Owing to the absence of rain in the region where Lima stands, and to the fact that an earthquake may be expected at any time, most of the houses are built of very light materials, because a strong building of brick or stone would be no protection during an earthquake.

Many of them are little more than large cages of canes plastered over with mud, and then made to imitate stone. The roofs are flat, because the absence of rain renders a sloping roof unnecessary; and even churches and large buildings that look strong and massive have really no foundation stronger than a number of poles and canes tied together.

Under a brisk shower, such as we often experience

on a summer afternoon, the whole city would melt
away, leaving only a mass of broken canes in a great
mud puddle.

Famous as Peru has always been for gold, and
silver, and diamonds, it has now another source of wealth
of which some of us have not often heard.

DIGGING THE GUANO.

This additional wealth is what is called guano—a
kind of manure, made by hundreds and thousands of
sea-birds. As we have heard, on the coast of Peru
there is scarcely any rain, so that instead of all the
matter left by sea-birds being washed away, it remains
on the spot where it has been dropped; and there, as

it lies year after year, it gets mixed up with eggs of
birds, dead birds, pieces of fish, and other things.

Hundreds of natives are employed collecting this
substance, which, when mixed with common soil, helps
to make seed grow and plants thrive; and for this

LOADING THE WAGGON.

reason it is sought for by farmers and agriculturists in
all parts of the world. The old Incas, it seems, knew
its value, for the very best guano has long come from
the Chincha Islands, about twelve miles from the coast
of Peru, and it is said that in olden times the birds of
those islands were protected with such care that it was

not lawful to land on the islands on pain of death, lest the birds should be frightened or driven from the coast; neither was it lawful to kill them at any time, either on the islands or elsewhere, also on pain of death.

Each island was, by order of the Incas, set apart for a particular province, and the guano was fairly divided, each village receiving a due portion.

At one time, all the guano sent to England was obtained from Peru, but now it is sent to us from other countries. At that time the people who sought for it were convicts, who had been sent out of their own country for having committed some crime.

The guano, often fifty or sixty feet thick, was shovelled out by these poor creatures, who then lifted it into an immense iron trough.

This trough was then emptied into a car, which, when full, was drawn along a tramway to the edge of the cliff, and there emptied, ready to be put into some vessel that was loading.

While the guano is being dug and loaded, a kind of salty dust flies from it, which is so strong that even the powerful negroes are obliged to put iron masks over their black faces, or they would be nearly suffocated; and the overseers, who superintend the workmen, live in houses made of iron. The poor labourers have to be satisfied with their little huts made of cane.

Strange to say, the guano districts, whence manure is sent to all parts of the world, are so destitute of moisture that scarcely any vegetation will thrive on their soil.

DISCHARGING A GUANO WAGGON.

D

CHAPTER V.

CHILI AND THE SILVER MINES.

CHILI is a long, narrow province, lying to the south of Peru, bounded on one side by lofty mountains, and on the other by the broad Pacific Ocean.

Its name, which means snow, is supposed to have been taken from the old Peruvian language; and certainly, to see some of the lofty summits of the Andes, crowned as they are with snow, the name appears to have been wisely chosen.

Who the first inhabitants were no one is able to tell us; like Peru, also, it has at different times been often invaded by Spanish soldiers, and after Pizarro had conquered Peru, his companion, Almagro, travelled southwards, and took possession of Chili.

The chief town is Santiago, a beautiful city with a broad road running through it from east to west,

VIEW OF SANTIAGO.

and in which stand many handsome houses and buildings of all kinds.

Both in Chili and in Peru the people have many
times been visited by earthquakes that have swallowed
up a number of them alive, with their houses and cattle,
but not very long ago, in the year 1863, a misfortune
quite as sad as an earthquake came upon the inhabitants of Santiago. A very important festival was
being held at the cathedral, which was decorated mag-
nificently for the occasion, and was filled with people
who had assembled within the walls to worship. By
some means or other, part of the gay ornaments took
fire, when, at the sight of the flames, the frightened
people rushed to the different entrances, crushing and
mangling each other by trying to make their exit.
The number who perished at the time is said to have
been between two and three thousand, chiefly women.
The poor creatures were either burnt to death, suffocated
by smoke, or killed by the falling stones and rafters.
On the spot, in place of the cathedral, now stands a
monument in memory of the awful event.

Before the Spaniards made their appearance at all
in the country, the old Incas from Peru had crossed
that great desert of Atacama, which, though so rich
in silver mines, is a terribly dreary place, and had taken
possession of as much territory as they could seize.
Owing to the absence of rain, the soil of this desert is so
dry and arid that no plants or vegetables will grow in
it. Fortunately a railway runs across its dreary waste
now; consequently, travellers who wish to cross it, need
not long be exposed to the misery that a long sojourn
would necessitate.

When Almagro arrived in Chili, he found a large

portion of it peopled by a tribe of Indians called Araucanians; and of all the red men in South America, these Araucanians seem to have been most determined not to let the Spaniards conquer them. They were a wild, warlike people, who loved horse-riding; and very clever riders they all were, both men and women. Their houses were merely wicker-work frames plastered with clay, and although they seemed happy enough—men, women, children, dogs, and horses, all huddled up together at night—Almagro and his friends no doubt thought it a miserable state of things.

It was lawful amongst them for a man to have as many wives as he liked, but as the rule also was that every day each wife should give to her husband a dish of food prepared at her own fire, the number of fires in each habitation was not unfrequently considerable. A polite way of asking a man what number of wives he was blessed with was to say, "How many fires have you?"

For their religious observances they required neither temple nor priest; all they did by way of worship was to sacrifice some animal under a particular tree in the forest which they considered sacred.

Like most ignorant people, they were highly super-stitious. They thought, for instance, that when one of their tribe died from any other cause than old age, some evil spirit had been at work; and before par-taking of food they always sprinkle on the ground a small quantity of whatever they had spread before them by way of gaining favour with the evil spirits.

A few of these bold, wild men are still left in Chili, and may be seen roaming happily about on the banks of rivers or in deserted villages. Their idea of freedom

is to be allowed to wander at will in any direction they
like, and they have the notion that people who dwell
in walled cities are slaves.

When they fought with the Spaniards they were
sadly puzzled to find out how gunpowder was made,
for they saw, of course, how useful it was to their

RAILWAY ACROSS THE DESERT OF ATACAMA.

enemies in battle; but what they actually did to discover
the secret you could never imagine.

They noticed that among the Spaniards were some
negro soldiers, whose colour, they thought, resembled
gunpowder. Consequently the first negro that was
taken prisoner by them they burnt alive, hoping that
they would obtain the precious gunpowder from his
ashes.

The land, like Peru, is rich in minerals, but, strange to say, many of these old Indians preferred for their own use either silver or copper rather than gold.

The working of these silver mines was terribly hard for the poor Indians a long time ago.   A law was

ARAUCANIAN INDIAN.

instituted amongst them, called *The Mita*, by which they were made to extract the precious metal, so that their masters might become rich, even though many of the poor miners lost their lives while doing so.

According to this law every Indian, from the age of

eighteen to fifty, was forced to labour in the mines for the space of six months, when, if still living, he would then be liberated for a few years.   Consequently many a poor Indian has had to leave his family, give up his trade, and go to a mine perhaps hundreds of miles away, because most of the silver mines are found at an immense height up the mountains, very near the limit of perpetual snow.   Therefore, in order to explore them, men and provisions have to be brought from a great distance.   Those mines which are lower down on a level with towns or villages are, of course, more easily explored.

The richest silver mine in Peru is at Potosi, but many of the Indians are made to work so hard, digging out these precious metals, that they have no doubt often wished the foreigners had never discovered them. Indeed, some of the American Indians are sly enough to keep the knowledge to themselves as to where certain mines are to be found, so that when they want any for their own use they can go alone secretly and take as much as they want.

There was once a wicked old monk in Peru who lost a large sum of money at the gaming-table, and so troubled was he in consequence that a great friend of his, an Indian, by way of consoling him, went and obtained for him a bag full of silver.   The selfish monk, instead of being satisfied, asked for more, then another bag, and another, and actually at last said he should like to see the mine where all the silver came from.   He was so eager in his request that his friend consented to gratify his curiosity; so one night the Indian, with two companions, went to the monk's house.   First of all they blindfolded him ; then, instead of letting him walk, they carried him in turns on their shoulders—how far the monk did not know—until at last he was put down on the ground and the bandage taken from his eyes. To his great delight he then found himself in a real mine, surrounded by large pieces of solid silver, of which he was told he might take as much as he liked.

The old monk filled his pockets to the utmost, and took in his arms and hands as much as they would hold, but, to his sorrow, instead of being allowed to walk home alone, he was blindfolded again and carried back as he had been taken; consequently, he had no idea of the route they had traversed. All at once it occurred to him that he would be as cunning as his friends; so he secretly unfastened a string of beads (or a rosary, as it is called) which he wore round his neck, and which he used for counting his prayers. These he dropped one by one occasionally, as he was being carried, thinking that when daylight came he could, by means of them, find his way back to the mine.

How mistaken he was remains to be seen. As he lay in bed, chuckling to himself at the thought of how rich he would very soon be, the Indian knocked at the door. "I have brought your beads, father," said he; "you dropped them on your way."

It is to be hoped the monk felt guilty for being so selfish.

In connection with Chili there was one man who, among others, did so much for his country that his name ought not to be forgotten. This was an Irishman called Ambrose Higgins, who was the son of a poor man, and who as a little boy had to carry letters to the post for a grand Irish lady. Fortunately for

CLUMP OF CACTI IN THE DESERT OF ATACAMA.

him, he had an uncle who was a clever priest, and
who, after educating his little nephew, sent him off
to the much-talked-of country that had just been discovered, nor caring much, probably, whether the little
fellow made his fortune there or was killed by the
natives; at any rate it was a dangerous experiment
to send a boy out alone into such a wild country.
For a little time Ambrose kept a little shop of some
kind near the cathedral, in the great city of Lima,
but finding that he had very little custom he left Peru
and went across to Chili, and there delighted some
of the authorities by the skill he displayed as an
engineer. He then bravely went among the savage
natives. Those whom he could not make his friends he
subdued, until the king was so pleased with the brave
stranger that he made him a colonel, and gave him the
title of Count of Ballenar.

From that time honours, won by his ability and
enterprise, were one after another presented to him until
at last, nineteen years after his first appearance in Peru
as a poor friendless boy, he was made Captain-General
of Chili; and it is pleasant to relate that he did not
forget, in the time of his prosperity, to send home to his
poor relations in Ireland a portion of his wealth.

So well did he occupy his high position, that even
now the people of Chili speak of him as one of the best
rulers they ever had.

At length, nine years after, he was made Viceroy
of Peru, dying, when quite an old man, after holding
the office for four years.

From all we hear of the good man he is certainly
one of those to whom the New World is indebted for
much of its present prosperity. His son, Bernardo, in

later years imitated the example of his noble father by
spending his strength in the service of his country,
although, in return for it all, he, like many other good
men, was repaid by his countrymen for his unselfishness
with ingratitude, and was even permitted to die in
exile.

Before leaving Chili we ought not to forget to
mention that the solitary abode of Robinson Crusoe
was on Juan Fernandez, an island belonging to Chili.
This island was discovered by a Spanish navigator called
Juan Fernandez, who gave to the place his own name,
and formed an establishment on it.

In later years a Scotchman, Alexander Selkirk by
name, lived on it alone for four years, and his adventures
are supposed to have given rise to Daniel De Foe's
interesting story of Robinson Crusoe.

CHAPTER VI.

BOLIVIA AND THE SLAVE-TRADE.

THE province of Bolivia is so called in honour of a great general called Bolivar, who made the inhabitants free from Spanish tyranny. Although a native of America, he was descended from high-born Spanish parents, and had been educated at Madrid. After travelling in many lands, he chose for his home the land of his birth, where, as he looked around and saw the amount of suffering that was being endured on all sides, he resolved that the work of his life should be to drive out the tyrants who had taken possession of the land, and make his countrymen free.

There is little doubt about the fact that these Spanish invaders, who, after the death of Columbus, poured into different parts of South America, were

hard task-masters.   They looked with envious eyes
upon the wealth that lay hidden in the mines of gold
and silver, and in order to enrich themselves with it
they employed the natives to dig it up for them,
making the poor creatures work so hard that their
lives were simply miserable.   According to the law
called *The Mita*, a cer-
tain number of Indians
were annually chosen by
lot for this purpose, and
those upon whom the
lot fell knew so well
what hardships were in
store for them that they
would quite as willingly
have received the sen-
tence of death.   Well
might they dread it so
much, for hundreds of
those poor miners per-
ished. How
they must
have wished
the Spa-
niards

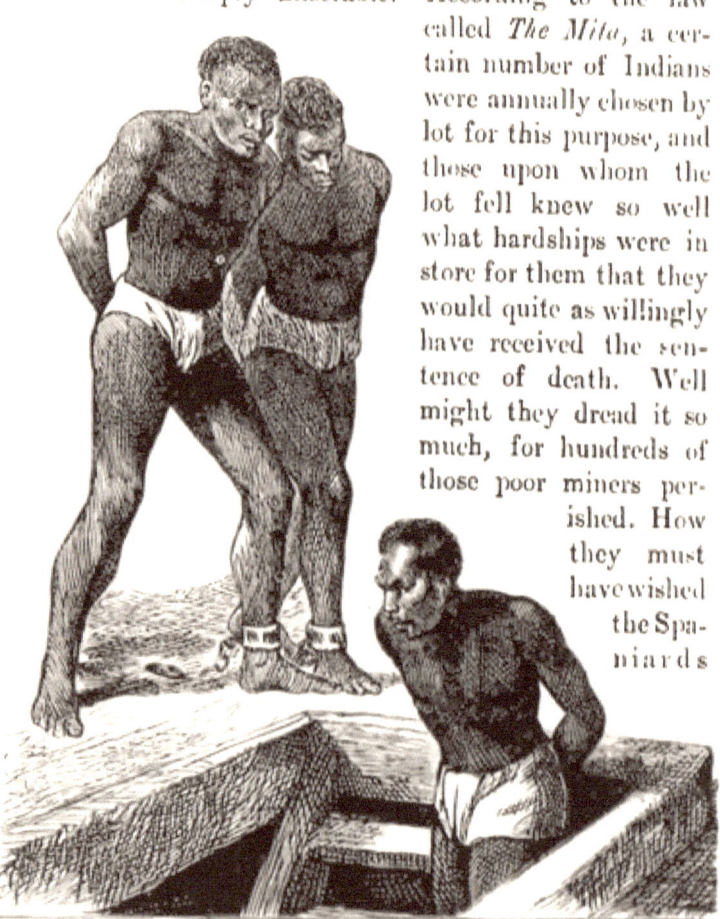

GOING ON BOARD SHIP.

had never set foot in their land, but left them in peace under the rule of their old Incas.

So eager were the Spaniards to enrich themselves, that they were not satisfied with having the natives only to work for them; they sent to Africa, and had a number of negroes packed off in ships like so many cattle, and they were made to work in the mines also. How horrible slavery is we know too well, both from the old Bible history of the Israelites who were in bondage to the cruel king Pharaoh, and from the narratives of the miseries formerly endured by slaves on the cotton plantations in the United States.

Very sad it is to read of the sufferings of these poor slaves. Very often they were beaten unmercifully by their Spanish masters for quite trifling offences, and were kept so hard at work in the mines that numbers of them died.

Not long ago in one part of Africa slaves were the chief articles of commerce, and were taken about chained together in couples, so that they had no chance of running away. In this miserable plight they were driven in large numbers before their masters, who generally were seated on camels, and who were provided with whips to lash the poor creatures if they did not keep up their proper speed. Thus they walked for miles until they arrived at the sea-coast, when they were sold to the highest bidder and shipped off to some far-off land, no one caring whether husbands were parted from their wives or children from their parents.

A SLAVE-OWNER.

Very often by the time they reached the coast their legs and feet were swollen with fatigue, while their poor bodies were thin and bony, for very little food was allowed them; and many of the poor little children were worn to skeletons with the hardships of the journey, and with the heavy burdens they had been made to carry.

As a proof of the inhumanity of some of those old slave-drivers, even horses were considered much more valuable than slaves. In the real negro country in Africa ten or fifteen slaves have been given in exchange for a fine horse, and the traders of slaves used to speak of them as we now hear farmers speak of their cattle.

Even in the ships, as they crossed the water from their own home, where they had probably been sold in exchange, not for money, but for iron,

toys, spirits, or salt, they were huddled together
in so little room, and were so miserably fed, that
many of them died there, and had to be thrown
overboard. It is almost difficult to say who were most
to be pitied, the masters or the slaves. Surely the

AT WORK ON A PLANTATION.

nature of those wretched slave-owners must have been
miserably hard and coarse, or they would not have been
able to treat as they did any of God's children. Some
of them, it seems, quite believed that American Indians
and negroes had no souls, and that they did not under-

E

stand what love, and joy, and suffering were, but were simply intended to be beasts of burden, like oxen, and dogs, and horses. Therefore they treated them as it is to be hoped any of us would be ashamed to treat a creature of any kind that God had made. For many years hundreds and thousands of slaves in America were thus made to toil, not in the mines only, but in cultivating sugar and coffee, or in doing anything else that it pleased the masters to command them to do. By degrees, however, as one sad tale after another reached the ears of good men in our own and in other countries, indignation filled many a heart, and not until a law had been made abolishing slavery were loving, humane men such as Wilberforce and Clarkson satisfied.

Now in no English colony are slaves to be found, and not very many anywhere else, because in most of the states the negroes have been allowed to purchase their liberty; consequently, at the present time great numbers of them who act as porters, drivers, and servants of every description, receive wages, and have thus learnt to be honest and industrious. The great day when the slaves were made free, after many long years of patient waiting and struggling on the part of all who hated slavery, was the 1st of August, 1838.

In Jamaica—a West Indian island that belongs to England—the negroes there were so rejoiced at the thought of being free that a great many did not go to bed the night before, but as soon as the sun rose bands of them were to be heard in the villages, calling out, "We're free! we're free!" Then they flocked to the chapels that had been built by missionaries, and thanked God for putting it into the hearts of civilised Christian men to loose from them their heavy bonds of slavery.

WEST INDIAN NEGROES GIVING THANKS FOR THEIR FREEDOM.

The white Spanish masters had tried for a long time
to persuade the negroes that they were little better than
the horses and llamas and mules of which they had the
charge ; but when the missionaries went to live amongst
them they told them that God loved all His dark-
skinned children quite as much as He loved the white
ones, and this was very joyful news to them.

At one time there was actually a law in existence
forbidding black people to enter a church or chapel ;
and very sad it was, we can imagine, to see standing at the doors a number of the poor creatures
who were not allowed to enter the place of worship.
We may be quite sure that those who refused them
entrance were of the same disposition as the Pharisee
who once stood in the Temple at Jerusalem, and thanked
God that he was not quite so wicked as other men.   As
you know, a little farther off stood a poor publican. who
was so sorry for his sins that he would not so much as
lift up his eyes to heaven, but smote upon his breast,
crying, " God be merciful to me, a sinner."   He, Jesus
tells us, was " justified rather than the other ; for every
one that exalteth himself shall be abased, and he that
humbleth himself shall be exalted."   Of one thing we
may be quite sure : that God would hear the prayers
of the negroes outside the church quite as distinctly as
any that were offered within.

Since the missionaries have taken such pains to
teach the negroes, they are much happier than they
once were, and among the sad tales that have come to
us are also amusing ones.

They are very fond of dressing themselves gaily in
bright showy colours, and the lady negroes like very much
to be seen in white muslin gowns, with gay ribbons and

parasols. All the negroes now have comfortable little
homes of their own, instead of having to exist in mud
huts, as they once did, and wearing nothing but coarse
ragged garments. All this is much pleasanter to think
of than the cruel days of old.

The following is one of the songs they used to be
sometimes heard singing :—

> " Oh ! poor negro, he will go,
> Some one day,
> Over the water and the snow,
> Far away ;
> Over the mountain big and high,
> Some one day,
> To that country in the sky,
> Far away.

> " Jesu Massa, bring me home
> Some one day ;
> Then I'll live with the Holy One,
> Far away ;
> Sin no more my heart make sore,
> Some one day ;
> I praise my Jesus evermore,
> Far away."

Although not a missionary, Bolivar was a brave
unselfish man, and it is to men like him that we are
indebted for the world being made better. Well does
he deserve to be remembered with love and gratitude by
the people who owe their present freedom to him.

He was a rich man, but instead of settling down, and
quietly enjoying his wealth, as he might have done, he
spent nearly all his money in the service of his country ;
and once, when a million dollars were presented to him
as a token of gratitude for what he had done, instead of

devoting the money to his own use, he purchased with it the liberty of a thousand slaves.

Before he died, too, he succeeded in making three South American countries, Colombia, Peru, and Bolivia free; and still it is said that he died in exile, and actually in want of the necessaries of life.

At Caraccas and at Lima—two South American towns—are monuments erected to his memory; so that where they stand, at any rate—and it is to be hoped in many other places also—his name will never be forgotten.

The history of Bolivia is very much like that of Peru; indeed, the countries lie so close together that Bolivia was at one time called Upper Peru. The chief town is Lucre, so called after another great general, who, like Bolivar, assisted in making the province free.

Potosi, another Bolivian town, has long been famous for its great wealth, because it is built at the foot of a high mountain in which are some large silver mines, accidentally discovered by an Indian in 1545.

It is said that this Indian, called Diego Icualea, was pursuing a vicuna on the mountain. As he was running, the path was so steep that he would have fallen if he had not caught hold of a shrub, which he seized and tore from the ground, when, to his astonishment, a quantity of silver was clinging to its roots. He meant to have kept the affair a secret; but the one person he had taken into his confidence (a slave) betrayed him, consequently the mine very soon became public property, while Diego himself gained little by it.

Many of the American mines are among the barren heights of the mountains. One method of carrying the metal down the steep paths is to put it on the back of an animal called the llama—a pretty creature, a little taller than a sheep, and covered with a short, dark, coarse wool.

It cannot travel quickly, but is very sure-footed, and although only an animal, is sufficiently sensible not to attempt to carry too great a burden.

THE LLAMA.

When it finds the weight on its back greater than it can bear, it lies down, and will not rise until its load has been lightened. So useful are these gentle-eyed animals (for each llama can carry a sack containing a hundred pounds of metal), that it would be difficult to carry on the mining business without them; and, fortunately, in Bolivia they are very plentiful.

CROSSING THE PAMPAS.

Troops of many hundreds of them may be seen in Peru, descending the mountains with their bags of barilla, as the powdered ore is called, each troup led by a horse, with a bell attached to his neck, to warn approaching travellers to stop at places where the road is not wide enough, or to avoid deep precipices.

In some parts of South America so many droves of mules and llamas cross the pampas, or treeless deserts, with loads of various kinds that the track is covered with bones of animals that have died either of fatigue or of hunger. To one of these places the name of "The Tombs" has been given. The care of all these animals provides occupation for very many of the red men in Bolivia.

CHAPTER VII.

BOLIVIA *(continued)*.

IN addition to its mineral wealth, Bolivia is rich in all kinds of plants and vegetables, fruits and herbs. One plant peculiar to that part of the world is called coca or cuca—a word we must not mistake for cocoa, because the Bolivian coca is not at all like the cocoa we drink in England.

In some places it is called spadic, and grows as high as six or eight feet, and has pretty thin oval leaves, which the Indians chew, on account, it is said, of the sustaining power contained in them. If we were to meet any of these Indians as we travelled in Bolivia or Peru, we should be sure to find them provided with a little leathern bag, filled with the dried leaves of the plant. This bag they hang by their side, and as soon as a feeling of hunger or weariness comes on, they take out a few leaves and chew them, and before long the traveller feels quite refreshed.

An Indian well supplied with these leaves can go on

working two or three days without food, neither will he feel sleepy; for there is some wonderful virtue in the leaves that banishes sleep as well as hunger.

Such must be the case, for the arrieros, as the mule leaders are called, always provide themselves with a good store of coca, when preparing themselves for a journey; and many of them think nothing of following the baggage mules for weeks together, day after day, from morning to night, running often as much as thirty or forty miles in one day.

There must therefore be some

A BOLIVIAN OF SPANISH DESCENT.

special virtue in the plant, although the flavour of it is so insipid that it has been compared by one traveller to that of well-boiled tea-leaves.

The old Peruvians, it seems, knew of the plant, and prized it, for we find they offered it as a sacrifice to their gods; and even at the present time the silver

GATHERING COCA.

miners throw sprays of it on the rock where they are working, in the belief that the leaves will soften the metal.

Of course we know well enough that the pretty delicate leaves have no effect upon the hard metal; though, at the same time, if the belief that it has such power makes the miner's work easy for him instead of being laborious, the little plant is not altogether useless.

Partly in Bolivia and partly in Peru is that wonderful lake of Titicaca, which is the largest and most important lake in South America. The principal attraction of it is that on the island of the same name is said to have lived the first Inca, Manco Capac, and his wife Mama Oello, of whom we have already heard.

There they dwelt before they set out on their errand of love, to instruct their fellow country people; from that time, therefore, the spot had been considered sacred by the Incas.

They bestowed great labour on the cultivation of its soil; they built terraces, and beautified it in every way they could imagine. The wheat that was grown in it was distributed among the different temples and convents of the kingdom, so that all might have the advantage of a few of the grains, that were almost as precious as if they had come direct from heaven.

These grains were carefully sown again, and the produce of them again distributed among the people, while a few ears were scattered among the grain stores, the impression being that they would purify and keep from corruption the food of the inhabitants.

It was also believed that the possession of a single grain of such precious wheat would ensure to its owner prosperity and plenty.

No wonder that a temple was built in such a holy place, one dedicated to the sun, something like the gorgeous sun temple that was built at Cuzco; and as every Peruvian was expected to visit the building at some time or other, and to present a gift, it became laden with treasures.

VIEW ON THE SHORE OF LAKE TITICACA.

When the country was conquered by the Spaniards, the natives, rather than see the sacred edifice robbed of its wealth, threw it all into the lake, and pulled the temple itself to the ground.

This island of Titicaca appears to have been regarded much in the same way as Mecca and Medina were by the Mahommedans, and as Jerusalem was by the Jews. Pilgrimages were made to it by the old Incas.

On the road to the temple were a number of huge rocks, which could be imagined to represent almost anything; just in the same way as we can sometimes see warriors and flocks of sheep in the red cinders, as we sit dreamily looking into the fire.

The Incas said these rocks were men who, as a punishment for not having fasted sufficiently, or made every necessary preparation for the pilgrimage, had been turned into stone, and were doomed therefore to stand in future as warnings for others not to neglect their duty.

There is another spot in this sacred lake which has been, and perhaps still is, an object of interest as great as any other in South America, and that is the piece of ground where now stand the ruins of Tiahuanuco. Travellers who have visited them tell us that they must have been built long before any other monuments in America—before even the time of the first Incas; and that, although so long ago, the people who erected them must have been very clever and industrious.

When the Spaniards went sweeping into that part of the country to take possession of it, they gazed in astonishment at these marvellous structures, and asked the Indians what they were, and who built them.

" They existed," said the poor red men, "before the sun

shone in the heavens, and were raised by giants; or perhaps" (they added) "they are the remains of some wicked people whom an angry god converted into stone for their wickedness." From what the Indians said it

RUINS OF THE TEMPLE OF THE SUN.

was very evident they were as ignorant of the origin of the ruins, near which they had lived all their lives, as were the foreign soldiers.

With all their skill these old builders, whoever they may have been, did not understand the use of mortar, or rather they could build so well without it that they did not need to know its use.

Like Solomon's Temple, the stones were made to fit exactly into each other, and were held in position by round holes drilled into the top and bottom of each stone at corresponding distances, into which were placed pins of bronze.

The position of these ruins, which evidently formed the temple where these ancient inhabitants used to worship, is not at all unlike the great stones that are to be seen in our own country on Salisbury Plain, and that we know by the name of Stonehenge, though differing from them in being much more accurately cut.

Then there seems to have been a fortress, and a palace, and a hall of justice; all of which prove that the place was the home of a set of people who were civilised and refined, but who, long before the time of Columbus or any other modern adventurer, had died, and left no sign to tell us truly who they were. For all that, no one can gaze upon these old ruins without being filled with admiration for the unknown architects who passed away so long ago.

The later inhabitants of Bolivia—those whom the first Spanish invaders found dwelling there—like all the native Indians of both North and South America, appear to have been quite a different race of beings in comparison with those old Incas.

Their days are spent in hunting for food and in decorating their bodies; and though some of them are partially civilised, there are still very many who live degraded selfish lives, and whose habits and customs are so unlike our own that we cannot help regarding them with curiosity as well as with pity.

F

The principal native tribes in this province of Bolivia are those called the Quichuas and the Aimaras, all of whom are very fanatical and superstitious. They wear what are called ponchas—loose blanket capes—and are generally to be seen chewing coca leaves while driving their mules, working in the mines, or attending to any other business.

Among other curious customs of theirs they practice one called the language of knots, which in times past was common among the old Incas in Peru, but which in the present time is almost a thing forgotten.

When the inhabitants of these regions had no alphabet, and consequently had no means of keeping a written record of their doings, they invented what was called the quipu—a twisted woollen cord—and, strange to say, they made this cord answer the purpose of a memorandum book. How they did it we cannot tell, but upon the cord they tied a number of threads of all colours, every thread having some particular meaning; and though no one understood it but themselves, there was quite a long history of events twined round the pretty-looking cord.

It was, of course, a very poor substitute for writing; still it was a little better than having to trust entirely to memory, and in some parts of Bolivia the quipu is still in use.

These natives of Bolivia (by the natives we mean, not the descendants of Spaniards who at one time conquered the country, but the real inhabitants of the place), though dark-skinned and half-savage, are in a certain way expert and clever. They are very skilful with the bow and arrow, with which they not only shoot wild animals and birds, but also fish; and another plan the fishermen adopt is to throw poison into the stream.

When the fishes take it they almost immediately die; then they rise to the surface of the water and are taken out.

Although the skin of these Indians is so dark that no doubt we should think it would be improved by being made lighter instead of still darker, they seem to have a different opinion. Their cheeks and round their eyes they paint red, and other parts of their body black. From the nose is often suspended a silver coin; round the neck

ANCIENT MONUMENTS.

is a string of beads or berries, and if room can be found for the gay feather of a bird, or for the claw of a bird or a wild animal, so much better pleased the red man is.

As a proof that they are rather proud of their appearance, they carry by their side a bag containing a few articles that they use when adorning themselves—a comb, for instance, made of the thongs of the palm-tree; a small quantity of a certain kind of juice to paint their cheeks; an apple of a peculiar description, which when

F 2

rubbed on the skin turns it black. There is also a pair of pincers, to pull out any hair that dares to make its appearance unnecessarily; but it will amuse you to hear of what the pincers are made, for they are nothing but two mussel-shells. They carry a snuff-box, too, made of a snail's shell, and a few other things; so that if detained from home for any length of time, the owner of the bag need suffer no inconvenience.

BOLIVIAN (SPANISH).

One tribe, called the Yuracaré Indians, who dwell in this district, though savage, are quite teachable and friendly. They make their home in one place among the plains or mountains for two or perhaps three years; by that time they are tired of the spot, or fancy they will find more game elsewhere, for they are famous hunters, so, gipsy-like, they pack up their things and march on.

One garment worn by them is a shirt made from the bark of a tree, which is cleverly constructed by beating the bark out until sufficiently thin.

With very bright colours extracted from various dye-yielding trees they then paint on the shirts all kinds of designs, some of which are quite clever and pretty.

The cacique, or chief of the tribe, wears on state occasions a pigtail made of gay feathers from birds, the backs of bright-coloured beetles, and shells of nuts; besides which both he and all the rest of the tribe paint small black stripes and rings on their arms and legs.

The Yuracarés are very fond of music, too, and comical instruments they use for their performances. For instance, the bone from a monkey's leg, or that of a stork, being hollow inside, is polished up and made into a flute or whistle; and though perhaps we might have difficulty in discovering either tune or harmony in the sounds produced by these bone instruments, the Yuracarés evidently wish for

BOLIVIAN (SPANISH).

nothing better. How delightful the noise must be we can imagine, when we know that the musicians, seated in a ring, play every one what note he likes, paying no regard to any one else.

The Quichuan Indians on feast days dress themselves in tigers' skins, and put macaw feathers among their thick bushy hair, when they are supposed to represent the wild animals of the forest.

This custom would lead us to suppose that, like some of the tribes in Hindostan, these South American Indians had once worshipped the tiger. At any rate, among the Yuracarés a strange tradition prevails about the tiger. There are two rivers in Bolivia called the Sacta and the Vio, which as they flow meet each other and unite. Just above the spot where they meet are three large stones, placed one above another in the form of a column about thirty yards high, dividing the river into two channels. The old tradition says that a tiger and one of these stones were the parents of the first human being, who was a woman, and whose name was Mamoré.

This Mamoré had two sons—one a bad man, who became the father of all wicked Bolivians, the other a good man, the father of good Bolivians like the Yuracarés themselves. The idea had no doubt been suggested to them by the Jesuit missionaries who went once from Spain to instruct the savages living in what they called the New World.

In many parts of Bolivia, and also in Peru, are to be seen also by travellers some remarkable buildings which are known by the name of chulpas. They vary in height; some are twenty others thirty feet high. Some are in ruins, some half-finished, and others as perfect as when first built.

They were most probably erected by the old Incas, or even by a race of people older still, to serve as tombs for dead friends; because in many of them skeletons have been found, as well as gold and silver ornaments, and other things.

They all differ from each other in some way; no two are alike. The large handsome ones are supposed to have been built for eminent and distinguished persons, the

GIGANTIC FIGURE AT TITICACA.

small ones for individuals of less importance; but in one respect they are all alike, and that is that the doors all face the east. The Incas, as we have heard, worshipped the sun, and most likely the doors have been thus placed out of respect to their deity. Although the present inhabitants can give us no certain information respecting these chulpas, an Indian guide once declared that according to tradition the builders, whoever they were, at the approach of death, caused themselves to be walled up without food, believing that by so doing a happy life in a future state would be ensured to them. Whether this statement be true or not is uncertain, but that the chulpas are among the most remarkable monuments of America is undeniable.

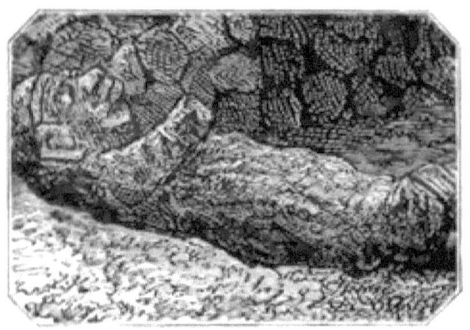

CHAPTER VIII.

BRAZIL AND ITS FORESTS.

THE large South American country of Brazil, famous for its ranges of lofty mountains, was discovered by Vincent Yanez Pincon, a Spaniard, one of the companions of Columbus.

Imitating his friend Christopher in his love of novelty and adventure, Pincon sailed along the coast until he reached the mighty river Amazon; there he stopped, and boldly marched into the interior to find out what kind of place it was where he had landed. A number of red men and women, some of whom were shooting at fish, others painting their bodies, and making necklaces for themselves of fishes' teeth and berries from the trees, stared at the intruder and his friends, and prepared to defend themselves if necessary.

Finding that the white men were harmless, however, they fortunately did them no harm; indeed, as Pincon, like most of the American adventurers of that time, was doubtless provided with presents for any savages he

VIEW AT THE MOUTH OF THE AMAZON.

might see, it is not at all unlikely that they helped them to load their ships with the monkeys and parrots, and Brazil wood that Pincon collected to take home to the King of Spain. Without stopping to do more than this, Pincon sailed home again, told the king what he

had seen, and, to prove his words, exhibited his pretty
parrots and all the other things he had with him.

Some years afterwards, a Portuguese commander of
a vessel, who really was on his way to India, was driven
to the same coast where Pineon had landed, and was as

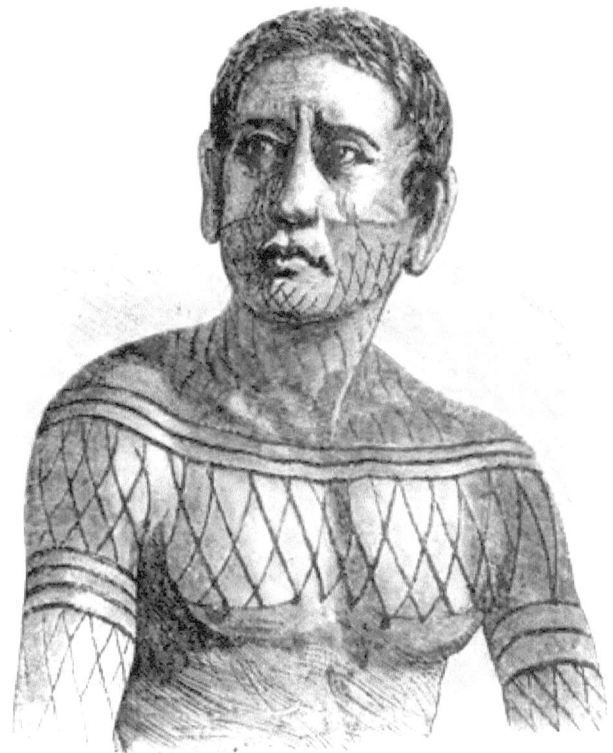

INDIAN OF THE AMAZON.

delighted with all he saw as his predecessor appeared to
have been, although, instead of remaining in the place,
he hurried off to the Indies, whither he had first been
bound.

After that there was a great deal of quarrelling

between Spain and Portugal as to which country had
the greater claim to the ownership of the newly discovered territory, all disturbances ending at last in
Brazil declaring its independence of either kingdom. It
will probably always be regarded as very closely connected with Portugal, because its emperor is a member
of the Portuguese royal family; still, it is really at the
present time an empire in its own right. To say very
much about Brazil would be impossible in a few pages,
because it is 2,600 miles long, and is therefore larger
than any other division of South America. So many
wonderful tales have been told of its inhabitants, and of
their beautiful home, that all we hear makes us only
long to know more.

Through the north of Brazil flows that immense
river the Amazon, which is the largest river in the
world, and which is so famed for its beauty.

Along its banks, stately, graceful trees, such as we in
England have never seen, wave their luxuriant branches.
Parrots, with lovely crimson and gold feathers, chatter
and gleam among them, and monkeys chase each other,
and gambol to their hearts' content.

The voyagers who have sailed down its lovely waters
tell us that as they lie in their hammocks, with the fine
fresh sea-breezes streaming in upon them, they are surrounded by some of the most beautiful pictures imaginable. There are to be seen numbers of little islands
covered with palm and other trees. So close to each other
some of these islands are, that a child standing on one
could easily throw a stone to another. Among them birds
with gaudy plumage are fluttering, while below them
numbers of flowers are thickly strewing the ground. The
scene altogether from the vessel is like one immense

dissolving view, for the reason that every minute the
picture changes.

Huts belonging to the natives are occasionally to be
seen on the water's edge, many of which, to preserve
them from being washed away, are well supported with
large stones.

How terrible it must be to be exposed to a storm on
this mighty river, we can form some idea from the
following story of two men who nearly lost their lives
during a tempest on the Amazon.

They were out on the waves when a frightful storm
overtook them; torrents of rain and hail poured down,
filling the boat, and so terrible was the tempest that
more than once they gave themselves up as lost. All at
once, like some good fairy making its appearance, one of
the boatmen spied a water-plant, and knowing, therefore, that they could not be struggling in very deep
water, he seized a very long, thick stick which they had
with them and plunged it into the billows.

Happily the stick rested in the soil beneath, when,
pushing it firmly down, the two men laid hold of it,
and by this means, as long as the storm lasted, they kept
their boat from being either overturned or washed away.

Tired indeed they must have been, for they passed
the whole night clutching the stick; and how welcome
daylight must have been, and the knowledge it
brought that the storm had nearly abated, we can well
imagine.

Sometimes during these heavy storms a whole island
is washed away in little more than a few minutes. It
happened once that some travellers, during a storm on the
Amazon, had fortunately taken shelter on an island so
full of high spreading palm trees that their branches

THE MAURITIA PALM.

formed quite a strong, spacious roof, and served as a protection from the storm.

Seated in their canoe, and while waiting for the storm to subside, the travellers actually saw this little island of Jahmna, which was three miles in length, entirely disappear. The tremendous waves rushed over it, swamping all the low trees and plants until nothing could be seen of them. Some very old trees that had stood the storms of many years struggled very hard for life. They appeared almost to be saying, " We and the tempest will try who are to be the conquerors;" but after a brave fight their roots were torn up, their graceful branches strewed hither and thither, and in a very few more minutes the waters roared over the spot just as if no island had ever stood there.

Of all South American trees, perhaps the palm-trees are as remarkable as any other in South America, for the Indians make use of them in so many ways that they are evidently regarded as an absolute necessity. They do not grow in every part of the country; miles of forests may be passed without a single palm being seen, while in other parts they grow in great numbers.

On river banks especially they abound, bending over the stream and waving their beautiful leaves in the breeze. There are very many different kinds of them; some are only a few feet high, called dwarf trees, while the great mauritia palms of the Amazon are more than 100 feet high. One traveller tells us that he measured one that was 192 feet high.

Some are stemless, consisting only of a spreading crown of large leaves, and one palm bears fruit that hangs in such large bunches that it requires more than one strong man to carry a single bunch.

The leaves of the trees are so large that the natives thatch their huts with them, and the leaf-stalks, often fifteen or twenty feet long, are used as rafters, or, when fastened together with pegs, form doors and shutters. In fact, there is a special kind of tree for almost every want of the red man; he has one for his bows and arrows, another for his blow-pipe, and one from the leaf of which he makes a cradle for his little black baby, a hat for himself, or even a wrapper.

At the entrance to the botanical gardens at Rio is to be seen a magnificent avenue of palm-trees, which, in reality, must be very grand; indeed, from the little illustration before us, we can form a very fair idea of its height and beauty.

Numberless articles of food also are produced from palms, such as bread, oil, sugar, salt, fruit, and vegetables. The famous betel nut chewed by the Malays is the fruit of what is called the areca palm; it is esteemed as highly by them as the coca leaf is by the Bolivians, the opium is by the Chinese, or as tobacco is by Europeans.

The cow-tree also we must not forget to speak about, for it is one of the largest of the forest monarchs, and is peculiar in appearance on account of its red ragged bark.

The fruit it bears is, we are told, very delicious, and is sold in the streets by the negro market-women, but what is most wonderful is that sweet milk is drawn from the wood, even from dry logs that have been standing for many days in the hot sun, though if left to stand long it becomes very thick, like glue; in fact, it is often used as a cement for mending crockery.

From another tree called the seringa we obtain that

AVENUE OF PALMS AT RIO.

G

useful substance called india-rubber. The men who are engaged in extracting the liquid earn very good wages for themselves, if they choose to work well and be industrious. They often begin very early in the morning, and the plan they adopt is to cut a hole in one tree after

SERVANTS' QUARTERS ON A BRAZILIAN PLANTATION.

another, leaving under each one a jar to catch the milky substance; so that in a few hours they are able to get quite a large quantity, all of which has to be dried in the sun before it is fit for use.

Hundreds of poor Indians build their huts close to

the banks of the river under the shade of the high trees, and gain their livelihood by collecting the sap.

With a sharp knife they split open the bark of the tree, when out flows the milky substance, which, when dried in the sun, makes india-rubber; the smoke-drying process by which it is hardened accounts for its black appearance as we see it.

At one time the provinces watered by the Amazon were called the country of the Amazones, though, strange to say, those great brave women called the Amazones who brought up their girls to be warriors, and either killed their boys or sent them away, did not live near this river Amazon, as we might have

EXTRACTING INDIA-RUBBER.

supposed, but in the far-off east. Many other lofty trees grace the banks of the Amazon, and not far from the coast are thick plantations of cocao trees, which supply us with the chocolate and cocoa we use.

Most of these plantations belong to rich Portuguese gentlemen, who have built for themselves handsome

OVERSEER OF A COFFEE PLANTATION.

houses along the river's banks, and who lead an easy, idle kind of life.

They keep plenty of black servants to attend to the plantations, and once a year, when the fruit is gathered, all are hard at work as we are at harvest time.

After being gathered the fruit has to be cut open, the pips are then taken out, dried in the sun, packed up, and put into ships that are bound for other lands.

Coffee, also, is very extensively grown in Brazil. It is said to have been first introduced there about the middle of the eighteenth century, and now in some of the Brazilian provinces immense forests of coffee-trees

NEGROES GATHERING COFFEE IN BRAZIL.

flourish, and the owners of them think there is no coffee in the world equal to theirs.

In order to make a coffee plantation, or a fazenda, as it is called, the owner first of all sows his seeds, and leaves the young plants for a whole year to develop. At the end of that time his servants gather them very carefully, and transplant them into another piece of ground, where, after being carefully tended for three years more, they begin to produce berries, bearing more and more every year, and sometimes as many as two crops in one year.

After doing this for thirty years, both the trees and the soil seem to have exhausted themselves, and new plantations have to be made.

On being gathered the berries are white, and have to be dried in the hot sun, or baked, before they receive the rich brown colour that is so familiar to us.

The whole of Brazil, in fact, is famous for the great size and number of its trees, most of which are made useful in some way or other by the natives.

There is one favourite nut-tree of the Indians that grows to the height of a hundred feet. In summer its branches are covered with rose-coloured leaves and white blossoms, and in autumn nuts as large as a cannon ball are hanging from its branches.

The Indians take the precaution of keeping away from these nut-trees during a storm; for if the fruit were to fall on the head of some unfortunate fellow, the result would be anything but agreeable, however thick and woolly his hair might be.

As a proof of the great size of these Brazilian trees, a traveller once saw a canoe that belonged to a missionary, and, although it was made out of a single tree, it measured thirty feet in length and five in breadth; and from a single trunk of the wild cotton-tree canoes have been built large enough to contain a hundred persons; while the leaf of a certain palm-tree affords a shade to five or six men.

It seems, however, that the strength of them is not

equal to their size
and beauty. Reared
in a warm climate,
they are like hot-
house plants; and,
unlike our English
oak, that is so strong
and so deeply-rooted
that it can stand
erect in a furious
tempest, these grace-
ful foreign trees, with
their roots extending
only a little way
below the surface of
the earth, are often
blown down by a
strong breeze; and
as they fall they
frequently destroy
many others with
them.

Round some of
the large trees
grow parasitical or
climbing plants,
called lianes,
the branches of
which twine round
the trunks of large
trees, forming very
often perfect gal-
leries or canopies of

LIANES ROUND THE TRUNK OF A TREE.

flowers; though in some parts these parasitical plants grow so thickly that the forests are rendered impassable by them, and their tendrils so cover the tops of the highest trees that all foliage and flowers but their own are almost entirely hidden.

These creepers twist round thick trunks of trees, and round slender stems, hanging sometimes in loops from the branches, or perhaps stretching themselves from tree to tree.

Where their root is, or how they grow, is quite a puzzle. As Topsy, who had been left to grow up as best she could, clung fondly to the new friends she found, so these wild climbers start up from some unknown corner and cling round the first shrubs or trees that happen to be near, clinging so tightly, too, that it is difficult to tear them away.

Some of them are slender and smooth, others are rugged and knotted. Very often a number of them are twined together, so as to form quite a thick cord, and are used by the Indians for cables, to bind the wooden anchors they use. Indeed, they are made to serve almost every purpose for which we should need a rope or chain. The Indians are so well acquainted with these forest ropes that when in want of one they take their choice among them, according to the use for which it is meant to be employed.

Some of them will bear twisting and tying, some will last longest in salt water, others in fresh water. With one kind the planks of boats, and even of large sailing vessels, are bound, and they are useful in numberless other ways.

When the branch of a tree falls, creepers are often left hanging in the air. If so, they blow about wildly

SCENE IN A BRAZILIAN FOREST.

for a little time, then, as if resolving not to despair because one friend has forsaken them, they throw out their tendrils and catch hold of other trees growing beneath them, and round these they are very soon as tightly clasped as they were round their lost friends.

As if to prove their gratitude for the support given them, they sometimes burst out into lovely blossoms, thus ornamenting with delicate tinted flowers tall, strong, stately trees upon which nothing but leaves are ever seen; but, strange to say, in the shade of the forest the climbers flower very rarely.

Hundreds of other trees also are to be found in those grand forests, all of which are made useful in one way or another by the inhabitants; and not to them only are all these trees useful, for we also, who live so far away, derive untold benefits from the vast wooden treasure-houses of South America.

CHAPTER IX.

MORE ABOUT BRAZIL.

AMONG the other sources of wealth in Brazil we must not forget to mention the diamonds, which, since the time of Columbus, have filled many a heart with envy.

The finding of these precious stones was, of course, no new discovery. Solomon's Temple was ornamented with precious stones; and faithful Job, in one of his parables, says, "Surely there is a vein for the silver, and a place for gold where they fine it. Iron is taken out of the earth, and brass is molten out of the stone."

Those old Israelites, it seems, who lived in the East knew where to dig for hidden treasure just as well as the inhabitants of the New World, who were as eager to enrich themselves with it as if they had been the first miners who had ever taken hammer in hand.

It happened at that time, as some miners were out

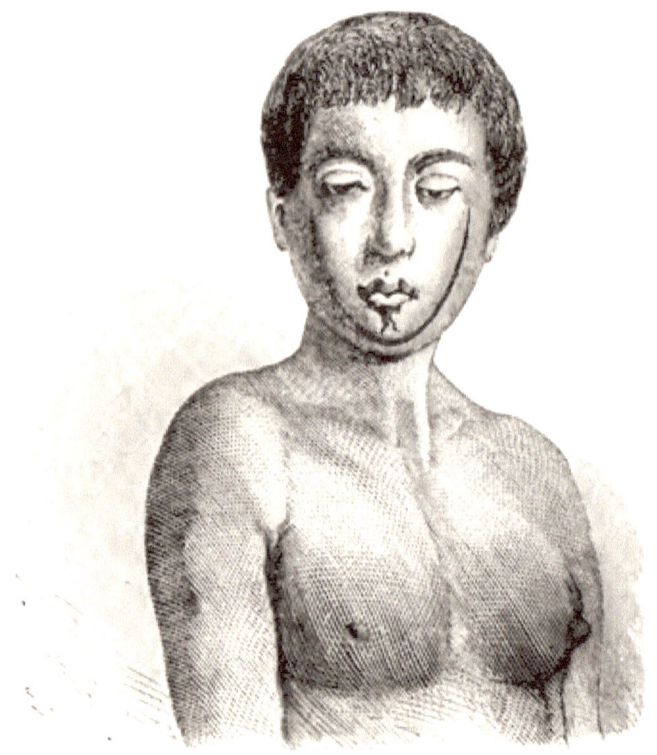

NATIVE OF BRAZIL.

one day in search of some of the marvellous riches that they had heard were to be found among the rugged mountains, they spied some bright, clear stones, which looked so pretty that they picked them up, and took them to the governor of the town.

He, it seems, admired them also ; but, little thinking
they were what could be exchanged for hundreds or
perhaps thousands of pounds, only used them as card
counters.

NATIVE OF BRAZIL.

The fact was these miners had been searching for
gold in what is now known as the diamond district, and
the curious bright crystals they had found were precious diamonds.   Before long the uncommon pebbles
were sent to Lisbon, and from there sent again to

Holland, where a learned lapidary pronounced them to be diamonds of great value.

Year after year the little brilliants had lain in their watery beds unmolested and uncared for. The red men had always been too busy shooting fish, waging war with their enemies, or hunting for wild animals to have time to pick up pebbles. What they wanted was food to satisfy their hunger. As was the case with those poor savages, so it is with us often. We leave what is really true and valuable for others wiser than ourselves to appropriate, while we content ourselves with what is paltry and worthless, just for the sake of satisfying our immediate wants. If any of us wish to have true riches, we must take care not to make the mistake of selling our birthright, as the impulsive Esau did of old. He foolishly consented to take a lower place in life than his younger brother, just for the sake of his dinner one day. Let us all try to keep our vision clear, so that when pearls and diamonds lie at our feet we may not overlook them, and, passing them by, choose only common stones and pebbles.

Slaves were generally employed to search for Brazilian diamonds; and even if the poor creatures knew their value it would almost have been as much as their life was worth to sell one. A searcher found guilty of such a crime would most likely either be beaten or thrown into a horrid dungeon. What the slaves did was to vie with each other who could find the largest stone to present to his master, and if one were fortunate enough to pick up what was called an octavo (a diamond weighing seventeen carats and a half) he had his freedom presented to him, and was carried by a number of slaves to the master, bearing on his head a crown of flowers.

The places where diamonds are found are in low ground on the banks of rivers, and also in hollows and streams at the very top of some of the highest mountains; and each diamond is covered by what is called its cascalho—a kind of thick earthy matter.

In diamond districts certain kinds of minerals are found also, such as yellow crystal (round pieces of blue quartz), and a fine slaty flinty mineral. When the slaves, therefore, who were seeking for the sparkling treasures came upon such minerals, they knew that diamonds were not far off, and began their work with a good will.

The plan generally adopted by diamond seekers is first to dig until the stratum is reached called cascalho, which is a gravel composed chiefly of quartz and fragments of different rocks of the neighbourhood, mixed with a reddish clay, and near which diamonds are always found. The washers then seat themselves by a pond or a running stream, and each puts a portion of this gravel in a wooden bowl, with which every one is supplied; then, mixing it with water, he shakes the contents, so that the muddy water escapes and the gravel and sand remain.

What is left is then passed through a sieve, which separates the larger gravel from the smaller, when the pebbles are picked out, the diamonds selected, and passed over to the rightful owner of them.

Other precious stones are found in Brazil, and also gold; though, strange to say, surrounded as the inhabitants are by so much wealth, they are actually greatly lacking in a mineral with which we are supplied so plentifully, and that is salt. Perhaps, in order to really understand its full value, we should, like the unfortunate

BAY OF BOTAFOGO, RIO DE JANEIRO.

Brazilians, have to be deprived of it for a short time. In their country it is said that an amount of salt sufficient to cure an ox would cost three times the price of the animal itself. On one of the Brazilian rivers, called the Xacurutina, is a lake that produces a quantity of salt, and a constant struggle among the Indians is continually being carried on by way of deciding who can get the largest share of it. To make up for this deficiency the Indians extract salt from the ashes of the palm-tree, and when they cannot procure a sufficient quantity of it they season their food with red pepper.

Rio de Janeiro, the chief town of this large province, is a handsome sea-port, and travellers tell us there are few sights more magnificent than the prospect that lies before them as they approach its harbour. As ships sail into port immense mountain peaks of all shapes and sizes tower in the distance, which not only add to the beauty of the scene, but which serve as guides to navigators as they make preparations for landing.

Strange names the natives have given to some of these summits. There is the *Sugar-loaf*, the *Top-sail*, the *Hunchback*, and the *Two Brothers*, all which names we should, no doubt, think well chosen if we could see the mountains for ourselves. They are peaks of the great Organ mountains, some of which are seven or eight thousand feet high.

The city itself is greatly changed since the time of Pincon and Amerigo Vespucci, those companions of Columbus who were among Brazil's earliest visitors; indeed, if they could see it now they would hardly know the place. There are well-built houses, handsome churches, hotels and other buildings, large extensive gardens in which vegetables are grown, and at the Rio

H

Botanical Gardens
is a splendid avenue
of   mango-trees,
which   not   only
yield very delicious
fruit, but which
·end forth a fra-
grant   scent   so
strong that the air
for miles round is
diffused with it.

People   with
skins of all shades
are parading   up

NEGROES OF RIO.

and down the busy
streets. Wealthy
Portuguese gentle-
men may be seen
driving about in
their carriages,
driven by black
coachmen, who look
quite contented as
they   sit   perched
aloft, dressed in
their gay livery.
In addition to the
drivers, three or

four negroes are often mounted on mules and riding
behind the carriage, just by way of giving an air of
importance to the affair.

To see many of the negroes of Brazil and other parts

NEGRESSES OF RIO IN THE MARKET.

of South America, one would hardly believe that they
were strangers in a foreign land; or rather that their
fathers and mothers had been dragged like cattle from
their home in Africa to work for the white-skinned in-

H 2

VIEW OF BAHIA.

vaders who had taken possession of the newly-discovered
country.

In the busy streets, where buyers and sellers of
cotton, coffee, sugar, tobacco, and others articles of commerce are trading with each other, dozens of negroes
pace up and down, carrying great bales and bags of
goods, most of them laughing and talking to each other,
or singing their negro songs. The streets of this city
are so steep that the negroes generally poise their burdens cleverly on their heads; then, forming themselves in
a line, they set off running, singing as they go, as many
other happy people like to do when at work. At one
time the noise of these singing negroes was so great that
they were ordered to be quiet ; not for long though, the
masters found out that their work did not get done as
quickly with the quiet negroes as with the noisy ones,
so permission was given for the singing to be renewed.

Many of them have kind masters, who feed them
well and who do not overwork them ; therefore the poor
creatures are content and happy.

The Rio market is a famous place, and one that is
well deserving of a visit from travellers who wish to
gain information on Brazilian life. Numbers of negroes
are to be seen there busily selling their fresh fine fruit ;
oranges, vegetables, and flowers they exhibit in abundance.

The women of this negro race, who assemble in
great numbers in the market, are many of them quite
handsome and graceful women ; and, judging from the
proud independent air which the beauties assume, it is
evident that they are conscious of their charms. On
their heads they wear a high muslin turban, in addition
to which a gay-coloured shawl is thrown around their

shoulders in all kinds of fantastic styles. It is sometimes crossed over the breast, sometimes carelessly thrown over one shoulder; in fact, no white lady could excel these negro market-women in the skill they display in the arrangement of their shawls.

Another purpose to which these gay shawls are appropriated is for the benefit of the negro babies; for

THE EMPEROR'S PALACE AT PETROPOLIS.

the mothers have a plan of twisting them so as to form comfortable little cradles, in which the little creatures rock to and fro as happily as if they were by the fireside.

At one time Bahia, or San Salvador, as it is called, was the capital of the empire, and even now it is next in importance to Rio.

Situated in the grand Organ mountains is a lovely spot called Petropolis, where the Emperor of Brazil resides in his summer palace, and where many of the wealthy Brazilians resort during the hot season. Paths lined with beautiful palm-trees lead from the town in every direction, while ferns and magnificent flowers, such as we should consider rare, peep up on all sides; and to see them, as they gracefully bend their delicate leaves and tendrils in the gentle breeze, they look fit ornaments for any emperor's home.

Indeed, of all spots near Rio de Janeiro, Petropolis is the most lovely, and would serve as well as any for that fair land sought for by the little child who asks—

"Is it where the flower of the orange blows,
 And the fire-flies dance through the myrtle boughs?"

AMONG the mountainous regions and in the forests of South America many tribes of wild Indians are dwelling who are still in a state of uncivilisation, and who delight in acts of cruelty. Of these the Boticudos are the most savage, and although many efforts have been made to conquer them, they have never yet been subdued. One favourite custom of theirs is to make themselves still uglier than they are naturally, by tearing open their under-lips and ears, and inserting pieces of wood into the rents thus made.

A very remarkable circumstance to be noticed among most savages is the power they have of enduring pain. We often hear in our own country of good men and women, and even of children too, who are very patient under suffering, because they feel that it has been sent to them for some wise purpose; but that ignorant wild men like these poor Indians, who have no refinement, and do not act from high and noble motives, should impose upon themselves unnecessary suffering seems rather curious. These Brazilian Indians are particularly brave and strong, even while enduring excruciating pain. They never seem to lose their courage, and would much sooner rush straight on to their own destruction than turn their back on the enemy.

If any of us feel tempted to shrink from or to despise these half-wild creatures, let us remember the kind of life they lead.

Some of their homes are nothing better than miserable huts, where mothers, fathers, sisters, and brothers all huddle together, living much more as do the animals that they feed upon than as human beings, who were made to love each other. From childhood they grow up with the idea that happiness and greatness consist in the possession of bodily strength. The man who succeeds in killing the greatest number of wild animals, or even the greatest number of his own fellow-creatures, raises himself at once to the rank of hero. They do not understand that the truest bravery consists in resisting evil, because they have no true idea of what evil is, or what goodness is.

What religion they have teaches them that there are two gods—one a good god, the other a bad god. The good god the Indian thinks helps him in whatever he wishes to do, whether the action be good or bad. Supposing he were to succeed in killing his own child, he would say the good god had helped him to do so; instead of that, if he were prevented in an act of cruelty, he would say the bad god had been working against him. Warmth, food, and pleasure are supposed to come from the good god, while cold, pain, failure, hunger, and even death are thought to be sent by the bad god.

The South American Indians believe that the bad spirit is stronger than the good spirit, so they spend a great deal of time and thought in preventing his doing them any harm. They seem to hold the idea that by some means or other he must be kept in a good temper.

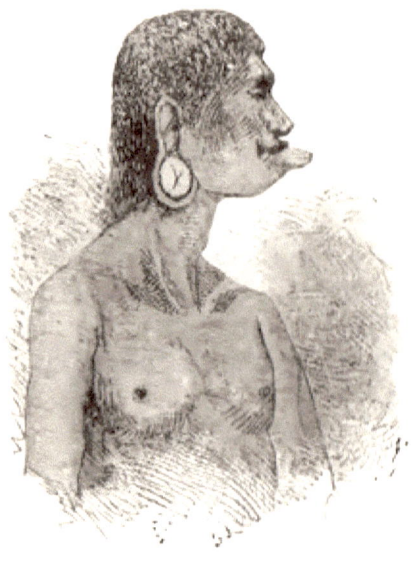

LOTICUDO INDIAN.

One precaution against evil, among many other very absurd ones adopted by the Indians, is to be supplied with what is called a medicine bag.

From its name we might be led to imagine that the bag contained physic of some kind, but the word medicine means to the Indian *mystery*, not *physic;* and certainly it is very mysterious that a bag made of the skin of some animal, as these bags always are, should have the power of charming away evil and danger.

Indian boys, therefore, as soon as they are about fifteen years of age, start out one day in search of some wild animal, which they must kill, and afterwards make their medicine bag of the skin. The size of the bag, perhaps, depends upon what animal happens to be chosen for the purpose; for the bags are of all sizes, and the skins of all kinds of animals are used—sometimes that of a buffalo, a wolf, or even of a rat. When the bag is once made, the boy is very careful not to lose it; for if he were to be so unfortunate he would have to be prepared for disasters of all kinds, and as to making a new one that would be out of the question.

Medicine bags are sometimes lost, of course, however careful the owners may be; but in such cases the unlucky person, who is not allowed to supply himself with a second new one, tries to steal one from an enemy, and if he should succeed in doing this he is looked upon with greater respect than he was before he lost his own.

Not only are there medicine bags among these Indians, but there are also what are called medicine men; and the title is one of very great honour, because it is only given to those of their number who prove themselves to be very wise or powerful.

It happens sometimes in their country that there is no rain for many days; so after waiting for a long time, until the people begin to fear there will be no harvest, one of them declares that he will make the rain come.

Accordingly, he goes up a high hill or mountain with a lance in his hand, and there he points to the clouds, pretending to pierce them, shouting to them all the time and entreating the rain to descend.

If when night comes there should still be no rain, some one else takes his place next day; and thus they go on until the rain descends, when the man whose turn came last in the business gains the title of medicine man, and is greatly honoured by all the rest.

Tales of this kind make us feel how ignorant the poor savages must be to believe such nonsense:—

There was a poor Indian who had been accidentally
shot, and as he lay dying his friends sent in haste for

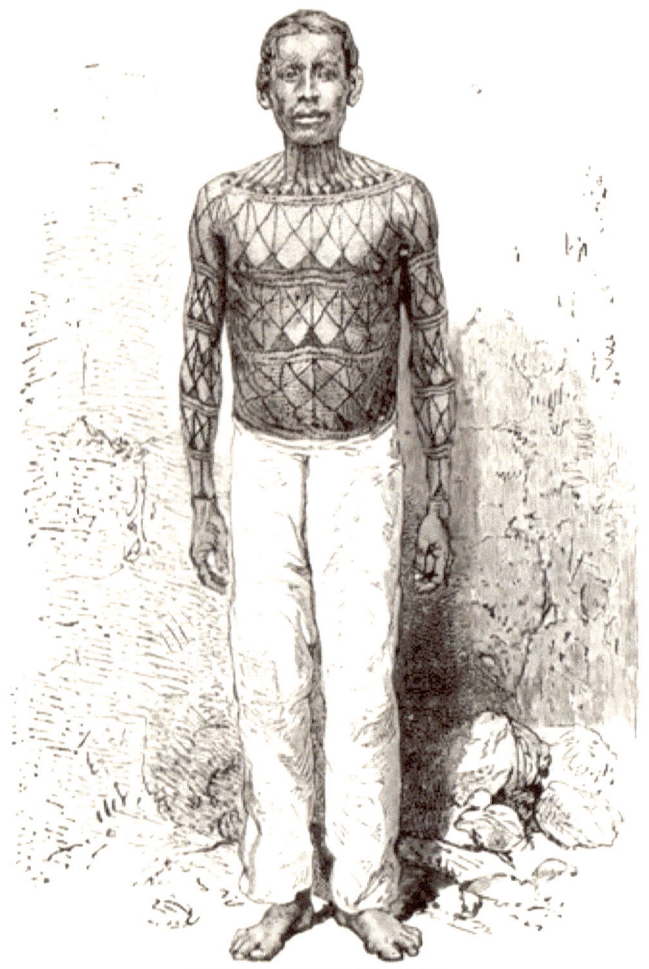

CIVILISED NATIVE OF BRAZIL.

the medicine man. On making his appearance he was
covered with the skin of a yellow bear, he had a bear's

face stuck over his own, and all kinds of strange things
were hanging about him—such as skins of snakes, hoofs

CIVILISED NATIVE WOMAN OF BRAZIL.

of deer, birds, bears' claws, animals' tongues, tails, and
teeth; in fact, he looked most frightful.

In one hand he held a rattle, made of a number of bones strung together, and which made a great noise as they knocked against each other; in the other hand he waved a spear, and as he approached the spot where the sufferer lay he grunted and growled like a real bear, jumping and frisking about in a very ridiculous manner.

Then, when he reached the Indian, instead of soothing or trying to cure the poor fellow, all he did was to drag the wounded man about.

Of course the sick man could not bear such rough treatment, therefore we are not surprised that in a few minutes he was dead; and though the friends standing round appeared quite satisfied with what had been done, it is difficult to discover any good that had been accomplished in any way by the wonderful medicine man. More difficult still is it to understand how special wisdom and power should be imagined to exist in a human being capable of acting so foolishly.

However, these savage tribes are gradually growing smaller in numbers; but the few of them that still remain in South America, especially the Botiendos, hate their conquerors, the Portuguese, and watch every opportunity of shooting at them or doing them harm in other ways. Like all selfish, quarrelsome people, they imagine that every man's hand is against them; therefore they regard all white men as their enemies.

Sometimes they hide among the trees, and cleverly send their arrows at any white travellers, or even at negroes; indeed, they hate the African negroes more than the white men, and whenever they can do so they both kill and eat them.

Many of these Indian tribes live in the treeless

regions, of which there are so many both in North and South America, as well as in Europe and Asia.

Either from fear or dislike of the white men who from time to time have arrived amongst them, most of the Indians have fled to the mountains and plains and forests, so that there, unmolested, they may lead the old life to which they have always been accustomed.

These treeless regions have different names given to them according to the places where they are found. In Asia they are called steppes, in the north of South America they are called llanos, in Brazil campos, in Peru pampas, and in North America prairies; but though named differently, they are very similar in character.

CHAPTER XI.

WILD ANIMALS IN BRAZIL.

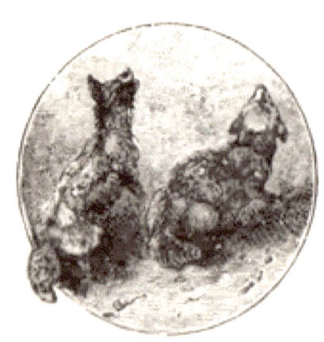

THERE is scarcely any country in the world where there are so many different kind of animals as in Brazil.

One of the most remarkable is the lazy sloth. Lazy these creatures are considered, because very often they are found in open daylight fast asleep, hanging to the boughs of trees; consequently the name of sloth has been given to them.

Still, the real truth of the matter is that they can move about quite quickly when so inclined; but, like the owl, they prefer night for their activity rather than daytime.

They belong to an order known among animals as

Edentata, because they have no front teeth ; but as they live upon vegetables, they manage to devour all the food they require with their back teeth.

Then there are the armadillos, which are covered, as many other **South American** animals are, with a hard bony crust not at all unlike a coat of armour in appearance. They eat vegetables and insects. There are several different kinds of armadillos, and nowhere but in South America are they to be found.

Related to the armadillo is the great ant-bear, which does so much mischief among the busy little ants. He is a lazy, unsociable animal, about four feet long, and with a tail longer than his body, and he has not a single tooth in his head ; consequently, although he is so large, he lives upon scarcely anything but ants, for the reason, of course, that they are so easily swallowed.

Other animals, both harmless and wild, are so numerous in Brazil that it would be a difficult matter to even mention them all.

First of all is the formidable jaguar or South American tiger ; then there are the tiger-cat, the puma, the red **wolf,** and the Brazilian fox, or wild dog.

Savage as the tiger must be, he seldom attacks man unless in self-defence, for the forests in which he prowls are so well supplied with game that he has rarely any occasion to lack food. If, however, the animal has once tasted human blood, he remains ever after a very dangerous enemy, because the memory of it is so pleasant to him that he always prefers it to any other.

The name given by the Indians to this man-eating tiger is *cebado,* and brave as travellers and hunters ought to be, the sight of one of these formidable creatures is enough to make the stoutest heart quail.

I

A traveller once said that the only time he remembered ever feeling really terrified was on one occasion when he was perched at the top of a large tree, at the foot of which lay a huge tiger with open jaws, ready to devour him the moment he descended. Fortunately the animal grew tired of waiting, so decided to seek a meal elsewhere, otherwise we should never have heard of either him or the traveller.

It is said that if a white man in company with a black man be met by a tiger, for some reason or other unknown to us, the black man will be chosen as the victim in preference to his white companion.

THE GREAT ARMADILLO.

All kinds of deer also inhabit the campos, together with our friends the armadillos and ant-eaters.

Monkeys are so numerous that the forests often resound with their screeches; indeed, very many of the monkeys that come to us are brought from South America. It seems that in their own country the comical animals are caught and treasured by the natives as pets, and not only so, but they are regarded as dainties for the table, and are often cooked and served for dinner and supper. By a tribe called the Sacandones, the aliiates, or great red monkeys, are eaten. On one

FIGHT BETWEEN A JAGUAR AND AN ANT-BEAR.

12

of them being asked by a white man why they did so, he replied, "Our ancestors killed and ate their enemies; but since the Spaniards, who are the strongest, have come, they do not allow us to continue this custom, so we eat these little men of the woods instead, whose flesh is quite as good."

Not only, though, do the forests resound with the monkey-calls, but with the cries of all the other animals. About the same hour of the night they all raise their voices together, and fill the forest with a very loud chorus.

A JAGUAR.

Some monks who once journeyed as missionaries on the shores of the Orinoco, before lying down to sleep at night used to pray for a quiet night and rest like that enjoyed by other mortals.

When the Europeans first landed in the place horses were unknown; now there are so many that they run wild on the plains, and any one who likes may have a horse of his own. It has been said, in fact, that beggars in Brazil go begging on horseback.

Fishermen ride into the water to cast their nets; bird-catchers are generally seen on horseback, galloping along with a noose at the end of a pole, to throw over the birds; so that if all this be true, horses must be indeed very plentiful. There are also large numbers of oxen and sheep.

Of course the birds of Brazil, as we well know, are famous for their beauty; numbers of them, dressed in red, green, and blue feathers, chatter among the branches, just as they did when Pizarro and his friends made their appearance amongst them.

We all remember the story of our good Saxon

King Edgar of old, who, instead of taking money from the kings of Scotland and Wales, whom he conquered, ordered them to send hunters into the woods to kill the wolves, who did so much mischief in England, so that at

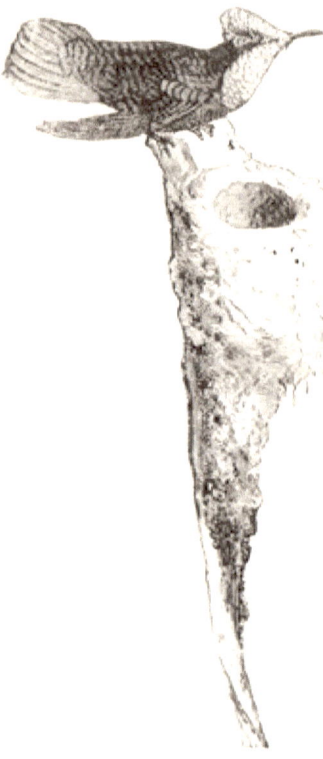

last all the wolves were destroyed, and the people were able to sleep comfortably in their beds at night. Well, it happened at one time in Guiana that jaguar's abounded just in the same way, and consequently one of the governors offered a large sum of money for every jaguar's head that was brought to him, and thus their number was greatly decreased.

The pretty toucan, with its red and yellow feathers, and the thousands of humming birds, all fly about joyously among the balmy, luxuriant trees. Then, to add still further to the beauty of the picture, the gayest of but-

HUMMING-BIRD AND NEST.

terflies flutter among the flowers, none prettier than those that have sky-blue wings, glittering like silver. Negroes are sent out with nets, fastened to the end of long poles, to catch these butterflies; and they are also provided with baskets for the flowers which they gather.

Other families of the insect tribe in South America are quite as well worthy of our notice as the lovely butterflies. The ants, and wasps, and bees may not be as brilliant in colour, but their little bodies are quite as

HUMMING BIRD.

beautifully made, and very wonderful are their ways. Little as they are, some of them are dreaded by men and animals almost as much as the large fierce forest beasts.

The ants called the ecitons are certainly not desirable companions for a traveller to meet. On the banks of the Amazon they are often seen travelling in dense columns of countless thousands through the pathways of the forest. There are two kinds of them, which resemble each other so closely that it requires attentive examination to distinguish them, and yet, though moving in the same woods and often crossing each other's tracks, their armies never unite.

Among both of them there are dwarfs not more than one-fifth of an inch in length, with small heads and jaws, and there are also giants half-an-inch in length, with very large heads and jaws, all belonging to the same brood.

The first intimation to the Indian that the tiresome little creatures are near him is a twittering and restless movement among some birds called ant-thrushes. If, on hearing this sound, he should attempt to go any further, he it sure to come to grief and find himself suddenly attacked by the minute savage biters. They swarm up his legs, each one driving its pincer-like jaws into his skin, and stinging with all its might. When they have once got hold of the poor fellow the only thing he can do is to pluck the insects off one by one, very likely in doing so pulling them in two, and leaving their heads and jaws sticking in his flesh, unless, of course, he has had at first the good sense to run away from them.

They are very fond of attacking wasps' nests, which are sometimes built on low shrubs. They succeed in cutting the nest completely to tatters in their search for the newly-hatched little wasps, and in carrying off their treasure it is quite amusing to see how sensibly they divide their loads. The dwarfs take the small pieces and the giants the heavy portions. Still it is not a case of

HANGING WASP'S NEST.

all work and no play, even with these industrious little insects. They are often to be seen indulging in what appears to be a real fit of idleness. They walk slowly about, gently brushing each other's limbs with their feet; but what is the most comical sight is to see them clean each other. An ant stretches out first one leg and then another to be brushed and washed by one of its companions, who accomplishes the task by passing the leg between its jaws, and then finishing the business by giving the limbs a friendly wipe.

Perhaps all this amusement, or whatever it may be, is as necessary to the busy little insects as a good game of cricket or blindman's-buff is to the girls and boys we know after a hard day's work at sums and geography, or Greek and Latin. At any rate, after a rest such as this the little creatures are quite ready to bite the next traveller who may happen to come in their way.

Another insect pest is a little fly, numbers of which follow canoes down the river, looking like so many thin clouds of smoke. They are each supplied with two little horny lancets, which they force into the skin in order to extract the blood; but there are so many of these tiresome insects in South America that it would be impossible to name them all.

In addition to all the other animals it has been found that at one time immense creatures larger than elephants existed in the so-called New World. As a proof of this fact, bones of them have been dug out of the earth or found in caves; indeed, a skeleton of the Megatherium (*a great beast*, as its name signifies) is to be seen in the British Museum by any of us who care to pay it a visit. It is impossible to judge of its exact shape from its skeleton only, but it certainly must have been larger than any animal we have living now. Its immense thigh-bone was three times as thick as that of the largest elephant, and its fore-feet was three feet in length.

Its whole length was eighteen feet; it had a small head, long neck, very large body, and an enormous tail. In its nature it seems to have resembled the sloth; its teeth grew in the same manner, and it lived upon vegetarian instead of upon animal food. It moved about, too, very slowly and heavily, although it was so powerful that it tore down trees as it passed along, or dug them up by their roots.

Another animal, called the Mylodon, also existed in those ancient forests, smaller than the Megatherium, but very much like it in many respects. The remains, too, of a very large monkey have been found. Indeed, it is very evident that long before the time of the Spaniards, or even of the very oldest Incas, a large portion of the world was inhabited by people and animals of which we shall probably never know anything.

CHAPTER XII.

GUIANA.

AT the north of the large province of Brazil lies a small country which, if we believe everything we are told by travellers, is like a swampy forest full of snakes, alligators, and tigers, and where the savages delight in eating ant-paste.

Other travellers tell us of its beauty; how magnificent are its trees and flowers, and that plants of different kinds grow in such profusion that they spring up not from the ground only, but from rocks, and stones, and from the trunks of trees. It may be that these plants are so anxious to help to adorn the place, or perhaps to know what is going on in the world around, that they take root and start up in strange places, where no one expects to see them, because they can find no room elsewhere.

Even the water in some places is covered with plants and flowers, so that it has the appearance of a lovely carpet. Indeed, it is no doubt owing to the great moisture of the region that trees and plants grow in such abundance; for, as we know, it is useless to look for lovely flowers or noble trees in the dry, arid soil of deserts.

In Guiana are large tracts of land called savannahs, which have become marshy by the overflowing of rivers.

Once every year, it seems, the rain continues for so long a time that all the rivers overflow, and the shrubs and trees look almost as if they were floating in water.

As we are told was the case in the old Bible days, when Noah made his wonderful ark, the tops of high trees at such times are converted into places of refuge, and not only men but animals are seen perched aloft among the branches, waiting patiently until the ground is dry again, so that they can wander about happily in search of their prey.

The native Indians think no more about these inundations than we should about a very heavy snow-storm or thunder-storm. They leisurely fix their hammocks on the top branch of some very high tree, and there they sleep as comfortably as we should on the softest of feather-beds.

No wonder that in times gone by the sight of a spot so lovely made foreign visitors imagine that at last they had found the long-talked-of *Land of Gold*, or *El-dorado*, as it was called; for in addition to the rich foliage and gay flowers, a number of savages were to be seen dressed in what looked very much like real gold. The fact was, the Indians had first covered their bodies with turtle fat, and had then stuck on spangles of mica, which presented a very gay, glittering appearance.

SIR WALTER RALEIGH.

It was in the reign of Queen Elizabeth that so many visitors set out in search of the golden country, all anxious to be the first to take the news to their sovereign that the wonderful place had been found.

Among the rest was the brave and gallant Sir Walter Raleigh, who, as we well know, once distinguished himself by throwing off his crimson velvet cloak and spreading it on the muddy pavement for his queen to step upon, rather than that she should soil her dainty shoes. Of course, after that day the queen treated him so graciously that he wanted to do some still nobler deed to prove himself a loyal subject.

The doing of one kind action generally leads to another; it is like the first taste of some delicious fruit, which creates a longing for more; so Sir Walter set out in search of the Golden Land.

It was all for no use, however; the Spaniards, who were already on the spot, would not let him land, and he had to return home again no richer than when he started.

Disappointed, of course, he was, we may be sure; for it was reported that some descendants of the good Manco, the founder of the Incas, hearing that greater wealth was to be found in Guiana than even in Peru or Mexico, had left their own country and were living near a lake called Parima, where immense quantities of gold were to be found.

On the banks of this lake it was said that a city stood, the houses of which were covered with plates of gold, and that in the royal palace, not only was every article imaginable made of gold, but that the king and princes had gold-dust sprinkled over their bodies, so that they were actually clothed in gold.

Costly as such a dress might be, it could not have been a very comfortable sleeping garment; so the princes used to wash off all the gold every evening, and were supplied with a new suit every morning. This comical tale originated very likely from the oil and mica dresses of which we have heard.

A SUGAR FACTORY.

After all this, we don't wonder that Guiana should become a bone of contention among the different visitors who found their way into it.

After Queen Elizabeth's death, Sir Walter Raleigh was sent out again to Guiana, where, he said, he felt sure here was a very rich gold mine.

He sailed out with a number of ships as far as the great river Orinoco, taking with him his eldest son, who was as pleased as his father at the idea of finding wealth for their country.

The second attempt was, however, little more success-

A VILLAGE IN FRENCH GUIANA.

ful than the first; all they did was to destroy a Spanish town, and in doing that the boy was killed.

Poor Raleigh did not live long afterwards. The Spanish Government complained to James about their town being destroyed, and he, by way of avoiding a

J

quarrel with Spain, ordered the brave adventurer to be executed.

After that, some Dutchmen were the first settlers we hear of in Guiana, and for a time they had a very pleasant time on the banks of the river Pomeroon.

But before long the Spaniards, who evidently had the idea that no nation had so great a right to any part of South America as they had, quarrelled with the Dutchmen, and took their homes from them.

Then the French tried what they could do to secure both land and riches for themselves, and the English did the same, until at last the whole country was divided into four parts, of which at the present time one belongs to England, one to Holland, one to France, and one to Brazil.

In British Guiana is the colony of Demerara; indeed, the whole of British Guiana is sometimes called Demerara.

It is from Demerara that a great deal of the sugar we use is sent, and hundreds of negroes and Indians are employed there working in the large sugar plantations.

Most of these plantations are situated near the banks of the principal rivers, which, as we hear, at certain times of the year are so swollen with the heavy rains that they overflow; consequently the negroes build high dams on both sides of the plantations, to protect them from being washed away, because on the other side are the swampy savannahs.

George Town is the capital of British Guiana, and consists of two or three streets, and not very far away is to be seen what is known as the Kaietur Fall, which is an immense cataract formed by a stream of water falling over a tremendous cliff 822 feet high.

KAIETUR FALLS.

There are many cataracts in different parts of America, but this Kaietur Fall is the highest of those in Guiana.

As in all South American towns in which settlements are made by civilised foreigners, the negroes and dark-coloured natives live in districts of their own, quite distinct from those occupied by the white people.

NEGRESS OF FRENCH GUIANA (SHOWING THE "MADRAS").

When at the very first the English people made their home in Guiana, the negroes took no trouble to adorn themselves with dress of any kind, but would wander about doing their daily work almost naked.

The masters and mistresses who employed them to do certain kinds of work insisted, therefore, that clothing should be worn by their servants, and in order to reconcile them to the new custom, would frequently give them old clothes of their own that they had done wearing.

Very comical it was sometimes to see the black women especially dressed in the garments with which they had been presented. The novelty of their appearance seemed at first only to amuse them, but by degrees, as the freshness of the affair wore away, they began to show the usual signs of womanly vanity, and would imitate the manners and appearance of their mistresses, imagining, no doubt, that they had succeeded in making themselves quite as attractive as any white lady.

Not only the women but the black men also looked very ludicrous dressed up in their masters' old clothes.

The common dress, however, now generally worn by

NEGRESSES OF DUTCH GUIANA.

the negresses and mulatto women is such as that in which we now see these dark ladies attired.

Their dress consists of a piece of stuff or muslin known by the name of gaule, folded gracefully round the body; and the peculiar head-dress worn by them consists of a handkerchief fastened turban-fashion round the head.

This *Madras*, as it is called, is so universally adopted by the natives of Guiana that it may almost be regarded as a national peculiarity, and yellow is the colour usually chosen for it—the colour of gold or of the sun—while in others are united all the colours of the rainbow, woven into gaudy and elaborate patterns.

A casual observer might imagine that there was but one method of arranging this gay head-dress, but in reality almost every wearer adopts a different style. The policeman puts on his turban one way, a soldier another, and ladies have so many different methods that it would be a very long time before we could understand them all.

The fact is, indeed, they arrange their Madras to suit the temper they happen to be in at the time. If they are feeling very sad, they give it a certain twist, which means " I am very miserable ; " if they are joyous, the handkerchief assumes another shape, which means " Look how happy I am ; " if they have been offended, another form is given to it, meant to imply " I am very angry." So that these head-dresses are really very useful articles of attire, as well as being what their owners consider them, exceedingly ornamental.

The natives of Guiana, like the rest of the South American Indians, are, although ignorant and savage, in some respects both clever and ingenious ; and as to bravery, like most other Indian tribes, they would never think of turning their back upon an enemy, or of trying to escape pain.

It once was the custom among one of their tribes, called the Caribs, of whom not very many now remain, that when a captain was chosen, in order to prove his powers of endurance he was for a certain time exposed to a mass of biting insects.

His suffering in consequence was intense; but if he bore it bravely, he was chosen as captain, and the rest of his tribe laid at his feet their bows and arrows, to show that they would henceforth obey his commands.

They believe that all created things came from the branch of a silk cotton tree, cut down by the Great Creator, excepting the white men, who sprang from the chips of a tree; they therefore are of little value.

They believe also that at one time there was somewhere a very large tree on which grew every kind of flower and fruit that has ever been known, and that all the flowers and fruit we have now came originally from that large tree.

The tree must have been gigantic; for they say that in the middle of it was a large reservoir of water, in which were all the fishes, and that one day a mischievous monkey amused himself by letting loose the water, and that consequently the world was flooded.

The love of finery is as strong in them as it was in their ancestors. Most of the Carib women wear, just above the knee, and above the ankle of each leg, a tight cotton strap painted red. This strap is put on in childhood, and as the girl grows is only taken off to be replaced by a new one; the result is that their legs

A CARIB INDIAN.

become ugly and unnatural, though the women themselves are very proud of them.

Another strange custom of theirs is to make a pin-
cushion of their lower lip, by sticking into it two or
three pins, which when they want to use, they take out,
and then put them back into the same place. At one
time, before they could get pins, they used thorns for
the purpose instead.

The cloth worn round the waist by the men is
sometimes long enough to be thrown over the shoulder,
and made to hang gracefully down the back. In that
case it is often ornamented with tassels, the owner at
the same time having his body painted gaudily, and
wearing on his head a crown of feathers, so that in
his own estimation at any rate his appearance is truly
magnificent.

When we hear that these Caribs at one time were
cannibals, and used to eat their enemies, we can't feel
very sorry that now they have become both less powerful and less numerous.

There are to be found on this coast great numbers of
turtles, which as an article of food the natives regard as
a very great delicacy. A very favourite occupation of
theirs is for a number of them to set out with their
steel-pointed arrows to the edge of the water, there to
lie in wait for turtles. They are so accustomed to the
business that, without waiting for the fish to make its
appearance, they can tell by the appearance of the water
the exact spot where one is quietly paddling along, and
often shoot their arrows quite a long way out exactly on
the turtle's shell.

By means of a long piece of twine fastened to the
arrow the Indian manages to draw the animal to shore,

when, if it should not be quite dead, he strikes it with a second arrow. The turtle pools abound sometimes with ugly red leeches, which fasten on the legs of the fishermen, much to their annoyance.

SHOOTING TURTLES.

Better still, however, than the turtles themselves are their eggs; and as each turtle lays about 120 eggs, there are plenty of them to be found, to say nothing about a great many that are not found by the fishermen owing to their being laid in places where they are not looked for.

The turtles lay their eggs by night, leaving the

water in vast crowds when nothing disturbs them, and crawling to a high part of the shore.

With their broad webbed paws they dig deep holes in the fine sand. One turtle goes first, and after making a pit about three feet deep, lays its eggs and covers them with sand.

Another then goes, and lays its eggs on the top of those of its companion, a third does the same, and so on, until the pit is full.

For a whole body of turtles to lay their eggs in this way it takes fourteen or fifteen days, and when all have done, the space where they have been at work (called by the Brazilians *taboliero*) is distinguishable from the rest of the ground only by the sand having a rather rougher appearance than usual.

After having laid their eggs they waddle back to the

MASHING TURTLE'S EGGS.

river, looking, when there is a great multitude of them,
like a great black cloud moving along the sands; and
down they tumble head first into the water.

The eggs are especially valuable on account of the
oil that is extracted from them, and which is used in
different parts of the country for lighting, for frying
fish, and other purposes.

First of all, the eggs, which are quite round, have a
leathery shell, and are a little larger than a hen's egg,
are thrown into a large tub, or perhaps an empty canoe,
and are mashed with wooden prongs.

Or, instead of that, sometimes naked Indians and
children jump into the mass and tread it down, besmear-
ing themselves with yolk, and making a scene anything
but pleasant.

The beating process finished, water is poured over
the mass, and it is left for a few hours to be heated
by the sun, when the oil separates and rises to the
surface.

With long spoons, made by tying large mussel shells
to the end of rods, the floating oil is then skimmed off,
and purified over the fire in copper kettles, when it is
ready for use.

The Indians say that at one time the waters teemed
as thickly with turtles as the air does now with
mosquitoes, in that part of the world; but, owing to so
much oil being made from the eggs, and also owing to
a great many of the newly hatched young ones being
eaten by vultures and alligators, there are not nearly so
many left as there used to be.

The Arawaks are another tribe in Guiana, who seem
to be a gentler race altogether than the Caribs, and
who still look back with horror to the time when the

Spaniards landed on their coast, and hunted their fore-fathers through the forests.

They are very skilful in the use of the bow and arrow, and in order to make their arrows more des-tructive, many Indians adopt the plan of tipping the points with poison.

They try to make strangers believe that the poison is made from the fangs of venomous snakes, because the effect produced by the poison is very much like a snake bite; besides which, the Indians are not very scrupulous about speaking the truth.

The fact is they dip the arrows into a liquid called wourali, a solution of the bark of a tree, and also beard the points, so that they are sure to adhere to the wounds. To prove how deadly the poison must be, a negro woman whose skin had only been grazed by one of the arrows died almost immediately afterwards, and even her infant too took the poison from her and died.

For killing small animals, or when the Indians wish to pounce upon their enemies secretly, instead of using the large poisoned arrows they make small arrows, one end of which they tip with poison, and round the other end they wind a tuft of cotton.

They then make a blow-pipe of a hollow reed, through which the small poisoned arrow is sent with so great a force, and with so direct an aim, that it seldom fails to effect certain death.

An Indian said once to one of our countrymen, "The blow-pipe is our gun, and the poisoned arrow is to us powder and shot."

Another kind of arrow used by the hunters, instead of being sharply pointed at the end, has a round head about as thick as a chestnut. Those of this description are used when parrots, little monkeys, or animals that are wanted to be captured alive, are pursued, because such a weapon merely stuns without killing.

The Indians have many quarrels among themselves and with the negroes who dwell near them, in addition to all the fighting that has taken place between their conquerors, the Spaniards, and themselves; so that although some of their weapons are very simple, they have learnt well how to defend themselves.

Another weapon formerly used by the Arawaks was a formidable-looking affair called a sapakana. It consisted of a broad blade of heavy hard wood, thick in the middle but with sharp edges.

The handle had cotton tied tightly round it, to enable the holder to have a firm grasp of it, and it was also made secure by having a loop of strong cotton fastened to it, which was slipped over the wrist of its owner.

These sapakanas were sometimes so large that both hands were required to hold them. A blow from one of them, therefore, must have been terrible. They are not often made for use now, but only as objects of curiosity.

Another Guianian tribe, called the Waraus, or Guaranos, though not perhaps so wild and warlike as the Caribs, are in some respects more savage and uncivilised. They are stout, happy, good-natured creatures, but very dirty and slovenly, and wear scarcely any clothing.

It is doubtful whether they would do work of any kind if they could possibly help it; but as they know they would die without food, they catch a great many fish by shooting at them, or sometimes by poisoning the

SHOOTING FISH.

water, and upon these they live, in addition to a few vegetables which they cultivate.

Sir Walter Raleigh, it seems, made friends with a few of the Waraus. He wrote some books of his travels once when he was in prison, and in one of them he mentions the Tivitasas—another name for the Waraus —and calls them a goodly people and very valiant.

In the dry summer-time they build their houses on the ground, but in winter they mount aloft and make dwellings in the high trees, on account of the heavy rains which they have between May and September.

Another tribe of Indians build houses in the trees, to avoid, not the water, but the tiresome mosquitoes that infest that part of the country. Whole villages of these houses built in the trees may sometimes be seen.

In spite of the character they have won for themselves of being idle, there must be a few workers amongst them to accomplish all the work we hear of their doing.

There are some very large canoes made by them, called woihakas, which they construct, not only for their own use, but for other tribes, or even for settlers from other countries.

Some of these canoes will hold fifty persons. They are fifty feet long and six feet broad, and if the makers of them were inclined so to do, they might make quite a little fortune for themselves ; but instead of doing that, the poor creatures, who know no better, very quickly squander all they gain, until hunger reminds them that they must return to their canoe-building.

Living as they do, it is doubtful whether these poor Waraus could be taught to think and feel differently. Their lives are spent in seeking food to satisfy their hunger, and in contriving the rude habitations which they

make to shelter their almost naked bodies from the wind
and rain. They are surrounded with little that is re-
fining and elevating, excepting of course the broad blue
sky, the sun and stars, the mighty sea, and the trees
and flowers, all of which are silent teachers to every
human being who gazes upon them, if only the eyes of
the mind are not blinded, for then, of course, the lessons
they teach cannot be read distinctly; and what we hear
of the religion of these poor savages certainly proves to
us that they are miserably ignorant, and need all the
pity and help that good men can give them.

For many years English missionaries have laboured
in British Guiana, and are still doing all they can to
teach the Indians, and also the negroes, who once were
slaves there.

One of these missionaries who went to Guiana built
himself a hut on the banks of the river Pomeroon.
Following the example of the Indians, he did not make
his bed on the ground, but slung a hammock across
the ceiling of the hut, to escape being bitten by insects
or poisonous snakes; and there for some time his only
companion was a little negro boy, whom he had easily
persuaded to live with him, and who helped him to cook
and wash.

Of course he took care to teach the little fellow to
read and write, and would gladly have taught the child's
father also; but it was no easy work the missionaries took
upon themselves when they went amongst the natives
of the new land of gold and diamonds.

The missionaries were white men, and so also were
the invaders, the Spaniards, consequently all white men
alike were hated; indeed they were almost as much in
danger of losing their lives among these wild men as if

K

they had ventured into the forests where the jaguars
went prowling about.

One day, as the missionary sat in his hut, he saw a
number of Indians paddling their canoes down the river,
and he thought if they would only come near his hut he
would talk to them; but although they did not attempt
to do him any harm—perhaps because they saw what
friends he and the negro boy were—they went as far
away from him as they could.

Another day, however, a dreadful thunder-storm came
on, such a thunder-storm as we in England can scarcely
imagine, for we never have any so tremendous as they
are in South America; and the missionary invited some
Indians who were overtaken in it to take shelter in his
hut.

It might be that they were afraid of the thunder,
imagining, as some of them do, that it was the voice
of one of their gods expressing his anger towards
them. At all events, they accepted the invitation, and
while the thunder was rolling and the lightning flashing
outside, the missionary took the opportunity of telling
them that if they were willing to listen to him he could
teach them many things they had never heard before,
and which they would be much better and happier for
knowing.

They said they would like to be taught by him, and
if their chief gave his permission they would send their
children to his school, and they themselves would go to
his chapel and hear him preach.

On hearing this the good missionary said he would
pay a visit to the chief; so he paddled down the river
in his canoe to the hut where they said the chief lived,
and had a good long talk with him.

A VIEW IN FRENCH GUIANA.

K 2

Of course the missionaries have to learn the languages of the savages before they are able to talk to them, and so peculiar are some of the dialects that they often find the task no easy one.

Our Guiana missionary friend, however, pleased the Indian chief so much that he not only gave permission to his followers to attend the chapel that had been built, but he sent his own two sons to attend the school; and by degrees others followed their example, until the missionary had quite a large congregation of black hearers and a school full of little black pupils.

Many other brave men have acted just in the same way, and have been rewarded for all their patience and self-denial by seeing hundreds of their dark-skinned fellow creatures abandon their old life of ignorance and selfishness, and, instead of it, begin the better life of purity and goodness.

Indeed, it is quite true that many of those poor Indians, who as some people have imagined had hearts as black and as hard as their skin, have been made to shed tears of love and sorrow when listening to the story of our blessed Master; and without framing any excuse for delay (as one of the disciples of Christ did of old), they have joyfully tried to follow in the footsteps of Him who so many years ago gave to the world that loving command, " Go ye into all the world and preach the Gospel to every creature."

CHAPTER XIII.

VENEZUELA.

VENEZUELA, or Little Venice, which is situated close to Guiana, is the most northerly of all the South American provinces, and was so named, it seems, because some of the earliest visitors who landed on its coast found a number of Indians living in huts built on poles in the water.

The sight reminded them of Italian life, so they gave the place the name of Venezuela; though if they had only waited a little until they had seen more of the place they would have found little resemblance between the two countries.

About the same time a Spanish adventurer called Cristoval Guerra set out with the object of finding pearls, for he had been told there were so many of them in Venezuela that any one might soon become rich who cared to go in search of them; but, brave as he was, he was so much alarmed by the fierce looks and savage ways of the natives that he was quite glad to return home to Spain without his pearls, feeling only too thankful that the black men had not taken his life.

A VILLAGE BUILT ON PILES.

In later times, when Bolivar paid a visit to Venezuela, he was crossing one of the savannahs with a companion, when some savage fish, called caribes, jumped into the boat and bit them.

"Put back the boat," cried Bolivar, as he felt the sharp strong teeth of a fish piercing his leg; "even the fish are savage in this country."

No doubt, on reaching home, Cristoval gave a most alarming account of all he had seen, by way of excusing himself for returning empty-handed, but instead of being deterred by his reports, other Spaniards started on the same errand; for in old times, just as much as now, people were always to be found ready to leave home and friends in search of wealth.

Numbers of avaricious Spaniards might have been seen from time to time trying to make friends with the natives, who very often had to be coaxed and humoured before they would consent to the strange white men taking up their abode, even for a short time, amongst them. The visitors, who were of course provided with fire-arms and weapons, took care also to be supplied with presents to offer to the natives; and very comical it must have been sometimes to see them bring out paltry articles such as glass beads and bits of metal, all of which delighted the savages. In exchange for them they gave the Spaniards real pearls, gold, food, and other things that were of much greater value; but of course the best of the transaction was that a feeling of friendship was created between the givers and the receivers of all the presents.

If only such a feeling of friendship could have been kept up in succeeding years, we should not have had to listen to the many sad tales we have heard of—war and bloodshed and cruelty—connected not only with Venezuela but with many other places in South America.

Before long the Spaniards arrived in such numbers that they became masters of the place, instead of visitors only, and then, sad to say, they did not use wisely the power of which they found themselves possessed.

They became tyrannical over the natives, made

servants of them, and, indeed, treated them with such
cruelty that numbers of them died.

Besides that, the Spaniards quarrelled among themselves.   They all tried to excel each other in their search
for wealth, and some of them, believing the tales told
them by the natives of a land still further off than any
they had then seen, where innumerable riches were to be
found, were only incited to still further enterprise, in
spite very often of sickness, hunger, and all kinds of
misery.

In fact, Venezuela, like all other places in South
America where Spaniards had planted their feet, was a
long-continued scene of dispute between the Indians
and their invaders ; and though it was not without a
struggle the natives gave up their liberty, the Spaniards
were the conquerors in the end.

How brave some of those old Indians were, we can
form some idea from the account we have of the conduct
of one of their chiefs, called Socoraymo.

He and three companions were taken prisoners by a
Spanish soldier, called Garcia Gonzales, who was so much
annoyed at the arrows aimed by the Indians among his
men that he threatened his four prisoners with death
unless they commanded that the firing should cease.

True to his kindred, the Indian refused to take the
part of the Spaniards whom he hated, and boldly called
to his countrymen to continue their shooting, apparently
heedless that in doing so he risked his own life.

Garcia, the Spaniard, could not help admiring the
display of so much bravery in an Indian, and if it had
been in his power he would have spared his life ; but
his soldiers willed it differently, and secretly carried out
their captain's threat.

RIVER SCENE IN VENEZUELA.

One traveller, who knows perhaps as much of Vene-zuela as any other, tells us that it really contains three great regions. First come the Paramos, or Cold Deserts, where keen winds blow; so bitter are they that whole regiments of soldiers have died of starvation as they marched along. Then there are the mountain districts, among which are rich valleys, where coffee, sugar, cotton, and other things are cultivated; and the last, though most important, division is Guayana, which was one of the places visited by our friend Sir Walter Raleigh when he was, as we have heard, seeking for the city of El-dorado. He said about it, " The country is so healthfulle, as one hundred persons and more were every day almost melted with heat in rowing and marching, and suddenly wet againe with great showers, and did eate of all sorts of cor-rupt fruits, and made meales of fresh fish without season-ing, of tortugas, of lagartos, and of all sorts good and bad, without either order or messure, and besides lodged in the open ayre every night. Still we lost not any one, nor had one ill-disposed to my knowledge, nor found anie calentura, or either of those pestilent diseases which dwell in all hot regions, and so nere the equinoctiall line."

One part of Guayana, called the State of Apure, is inhabited by a race of people called the Llaneros, who are considered the best horsemen in America. One of their countrymen, called Ramon Paez, says of them that, "Cast upon a wild and apparently interminable plain, the domain of savage beasts and poisonous reptiles, their lot is to pass all their life in a perpetual struggle, not only with the primitive possessors of the land, but with the elements themselves—often as fierce as they are grand."

These Llaneros need truly to be a strong, hardy set of

men, for the fact is that in Apure from April to August the rain falls so heavily and so continuously that during most of that time the whole country is little better than one vast lake, and many of the natives and cattle that are not drowned in the waters are destroyed by alligators or by the savage caribe fish that astonished and annoyed Bolivar so much.

In this part of the world are to be seen some immense water-lilies. So large they are that we could almost imagine they belonged to an ancient family of very large plants that ornamented the world in those ages long ago when the Megatherium and the Mylodon and such like huge creatures lived and stalked about among our forests and by the sides of our rivers. The place where the finest of the lilies grow is on the beautiful Lake Muna, the water of which, instead of being pure and clear, as we should think the home of such lovely flowers ought to be, is as black as ink.

Not very long ago, a gentleman who was travelling in this very region thought he should like to see the flowers for himself, then he would know whether all the reports were true that he had heard about them; so with two or three black servants as guides, he got into a boat, and off they set in search of them.

Before they had gone far they were so fearfully teased by thick clouds of mosquitoes that the gentleman felt quite inclined to turn back again, but just as he had decided to do so, one of his servants called out "We are here;" and there sure enough a most gorgeous sight presented itself to their gaze.

The surface of the lake was thick with huge dark-green leaves, each of which had all round its edge a border of a wine-coloured rosy tint. Among these great

leaves expanded magnificent flowers, whose petals outside were milky white, while inside they were rose-

GIGANTIC WATER LILIES.

coloured, the very centre of the flower being a rich
violet tint.

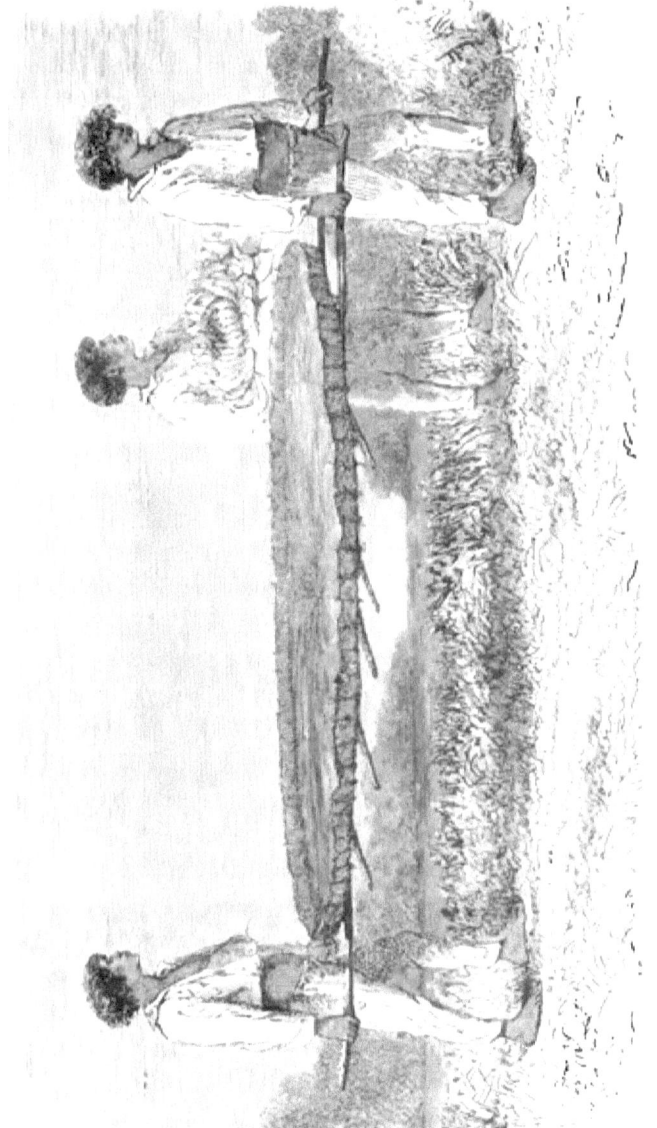

CARRYING THE LILY LEAF.

The surface of the lake looked like an immense flowery carpet, upon which were walking hundreds of wading birds, who trotted along perfectly at ease, knowing all of them that the ground beneath them was quite strong enough to bear the weight of their bodies, even though some of them were by no means small specimens of the bird family.

The next thing to be done was to gather one of the lilies, so in order to do this the boat was pushed into the huge net-work of leaves and flowers, and there, with the aid of a strong stick, a splendid lily, and also a bud were broken away from the rough, strong, prickly stalk. More difficult still was it to obtain one of the huge leaves, for they were held down by knotty stalks as thick as a ship's cable; but after a good deal of hard work a leaf also was broken off. Its size and shape you see by looking at the engraving.

Its weight was actually thirteen pounds and a half: the flower weighed three pounds and a half, and the bud weighed two pounds and a quarter. How carefully they are all being carried we can see. A kind of carriage for the leaf was made by fastening together a number of sticks which two black servants carried, the large flower and bud being carried by a third native.

The Indians of the upper Amazon have given the name of japna to this exquisite flower, because of the resemblance of its leaf to a great iron pan without a handle in which they cook their food. In the Amazon language this pan is called japuna.

In Brazil there is a certain bird of the name of Uaope, which perches on this lily leaf in search of insects, flies, and dragon-flies for its food; therefore the Indians call their pan and also the leaf of the lily after the bird.

CHAPTER XIV.

FROM COLOMBIA TO URUGUAY.

THE province next to Venezuela is that of Colombia,
or New Granada as it is also
called, and although we know that
now it is like other South American
countries, a land of beauty, it is
almost a marvel that we know
anything at all about its past history, for after the settlement of
its conquerors, the Spaniards, the
native Indians in the place decreased
so rapidly that there was scarcely any one left to tell all
the old tales and legends of the land.

To make matters still worse, the monks and priests
destroyed many of their temples and images in trying
to put down the old religion of the country, and
demolished, also, every stone or rock upon which their
hieroglyphics were inscribed; so that even the very
name of the Chibchas, as one of the chief tribes was
called, was nearly forgotten.

The tale handed down from father to son by these people was that one day, at a time when they were very savage and ignorant, without religion and without laws, an old grey-headed man with a long, white beard, made his appearance among them, and taught them to be industrious, and peaceable, and orderly. He taught them how to spin, and weave, and cultivate the ground, after which he disappeared.

The places where he had last been seen were then considered sacred by his followers, who tried after he had gone to do all that he had wished, and his memory was cherished by them with love.

After a good deal of searching among old writings, this little narrative and one or two others were brought to light; among them is an explanation of the beginning of the world.

At first these Chibchas say darkness reigned over the whole earth, the light was enclosed in a large space, out of which flew at last some enormous birds with fiery beaks.

One day, when thunder rolled and lightning flashed, a beautiful woman was seen to emerge from this region of light, carrying in her arms a little boy. When the little boy grew to be a man he married the beautiful woman, and after this the earth began to be inhabited by human beings. Then, after some years, the woman and her husband returned to the land of light.

At Bogota, a town in Colombia, is the wonderful water-fall of Tequendama, which is formed by the leaping of the stream at one bound over a precipice 475 feet in height. It was considered sacred by these old Chibchas, who offered sacrifices there in memory, they said, of a blow given by the beautiful woman with her wand

FALLS OF TEQUENDAMA.

I

when she opened this breach to save her people from
the deluge. The old Greeks, it seems, in the same way
gave thanks every year to Neptune for having opened a
passage in one of their rivers between two mountains.

Although really neither Neptune or the woman had
merited the thanks bestowed upon them, the people
themselves were both richer and happier for having

GAME DEALERS OF BOGOTA.

offered their sacrifices, and for having returned their
thanks.

The wealthiest of men is poor at heart who can
receive with a cold, indifferent spirit the thousand
blessings that he needs to supply his daily and hourly
wants, just as if they were all his by right, and thanks
from him were altogether unnecessary.

SCENE IN BOGOTA—STARTING ON A JOURNEY.

God, the only Giver of all mercies, smiles upon His
creatures, and acknowledges their thanks. It may be,
too, that thanks tendered in ignorance to some object
that He has made instead of to Himself are better than
no thanks at all. Far better it is for any of us to mistake the source of our benefits than to have hearts in-
capable of feeling grateful.

Quito, the capital of Ecuador, the province next to
Colombia, is the ancient capital of the Peruvian mon-
archy, and is one of the most remarkable cities of the
world, on account of its being situated so high above the
sea. Its cathedral is an object of great admiration. The
whole province of Ecuador, so well known for its terrible volcanoes and lofty mountains, is frequently called
Quito or Equator, because it is under the equinoctial
line.

The highest of the volcanoes is Cotopaxi, from
which at different times there have been eruptions,
when the cinders and fragments of rock sent out by it
have covered the valleys around to the extent of several
leagues.

In 1758 the flames of the volcano rose 2,700 feet
above the edge of the crater, and in 1744 the roaring
of the mountain was heard as far as Honda, six hundred
miles away. Another time, in 1768, the quantity of
cinders sent up from the mouth of the volcano was so
great that until mid-day the sky was darkened with
them.

After this, for twenty years it was quiet—just as
we should expect an angry man to be silent and ashamed
of himself after giving way to a fit of passion; then
it burst out again as furiously as before. The old
Mexicans gave the name of Popocatepetl, or "the Hill

that Smokes," to a volcano in their country, and looked upon it as a god. They had a mysterious dread of it,

THE GRAND ALTAR, CATHEDRAL OF QUITO.

and told the white strangers in whispers that no man could ascend its slopes and still live.

The Spaniards laughed on hearing this, and resolved to find out what there was to fear. Accordingly, ten of them began ascending the steep sides
of the mountain, taking with them as many Indians
as they could persuade to join them. On they all
went happily for some time, until they came to where

STREET SCENE IN QUITO.

no grass was seen growing, nor any trees, nor any
vegetation of any kind, but where strange noises were
heard like distant thunder. The Indians then looked
alarmed, and set off back again with all speed, thinking
to themselves how foolish the white men were to rush
as they were doing into such great danger. Left to
themselves, the ten brave Spaniards continued their
way, over the black, glazed sand, and through the chill-

ing air, until they reached the region of perpetual snow,
and found themselves among glittering, treacherous
glaciers and crevasses, and with huge slippery-pathed
precipices yawning around—a great change for them,
when it had been warm, bright summer not many hours
before at the foot of the volcano.

SOLDIER OF QUITO.   WATCHMAN OF QUITO.

All at once, however, a little higher still, they en-
countered such a fierce storm of cinders, and smoke, and
sparks that they rushed back again nearly suffocated;
and if not laughed at by the Indians, they confirmed
them, no doubt, in their belief that the volcano was a
mighty god.

Another time the Spaniards were in want of gun-powder, when a party of brave fellows, led by one called Francisco Montano, ascended the same volcano in search of sulphur—an important ingredient in the manufacture of gunpowder.

When they reached the top of the volcano, flame was actually issuing from the abyss, and, brave as they all were, no one could have wondered if they had dared to venture no farther. Not so, however. Men who, like these Spaniards, go in search of new countries have generally stout hearts; and though these sulphur-seekers knew that at any moment they might have been suffo-cated by flame or vapour, they persevered in the task they had undertaken.

In order to obtain the sulphur it was necessary that one of their number should be let down, by means of a basket, into the lurid crater. So lots were drawn, by way of deciding who should be the inmate of the basket, and the lot fell upon the leader, Francisco Montano.

As he bravely went down, the light shone on his face and steam rose around him; but without showing any fear (however much or little he may have felt), he hastily stretched out his hands and broke off from the sides of the crater as much of the bright yellow sub-stance as he could take with him, and was then drawn up again. Not once only did he descend, but several times, until he had obtained as much sulphur as he knew would be required.

After such an act of bravery the Indians must have thought that not only the volcano was a god, but that the brave Spaniard must be god-like also.

In Ecuador grows extensively the cinchona-tree, which yields the famous Peruvian bark or quinine. It is a very

GATHERING CINCHONA BARK.

large tree, bearing evergreen leaves, and also a pretty white and rose-coloured flower.

The bark of the tree has long been used in our country as a medicine, and in order to procure it a number of Indians are employed several months in the year.

A party of them start out together into the forests where it grows, and first of all build a number of little huts for themselves, which serve not only as sleeping-places, but as drying-sheds for the bark which they cut from the trees.

The trees are cut close to the ground, and stripped of every particle of bark, which, after being thoroughly dried, is folded first in woollen cloths, and afterwards in hides made from skins of animals; and thus in packages, each of which is called a drum, it is sent away to places where it is wanted.

Leaving Ecuador, to pay an imaginary visit to the southern province of **Paraguay**, we find ourselves in a country that in many respects is very similar to the countries of which we have already heard.

Like them, it has been the scene of much bloodshed. It was discovered by Sebastian Cabot in 1526, and after that was peopled by a number of Spaniards, who fought the Indians, as their countrymen had done elsewhere, and killed them, by way of establishing themselves as the rightful owners of the place.

For many years misery and cruelty abounded on all sides, because the men who possessed the right to rule, and who ought to have taught the people how to live good, useful lives, were bad, ambitious men, who cared for nothing but amassing wealth for themselves, and establishing their own power.

It is in this country, lying so far from the sea that

sea-breezes never reach it, that a kind of holly called the maté-tree grows, and from the leaves of which a liquor is made that is drunk all over the southern part of the continent as a substitute for tea and coffee.

There are large plantations of it, called yerbales, belonging to rich Spanish and Portuguese settlers, who employ a number of natives called Peons to work for them ; so that for six months in the year these poor fellows find plenty to do in collecting the leaves and twigs of the tree, drying them over a fire, and then beating them into small fragments, after which they pack them in large hide bags ready to be sent away.

When made, it is taken without milk or sugar, and by wealthy people it is sucked through a silver tube ; poor folks have, of course, to content themselves with a tube less costly.

In its effect upon the system maté is both refreshing and nourishing, and may for days be taken as a substitute for food.

Among the Indian tribes who inhabit Paraguay are the Canguas, or forest people, who live among the thick woods, and who appear to be harmless creatures, living very much to themselves, and subsisting on such animals as they may be able to kill with their bows and arrows. The Guayanas, another tribe, are sometimes sufficiently civilised to work in the yerbales among the other labourers, and are no doubt highly delighted to have a ride occasionally in the train that now runs through the lovely country.

In these Paraguayan trains two carriages like these shown in the picture are reserved for the poor black folk, and the rows of black legs would be a very laughable sight to us, could we see them.

PARAGUAYAN INDIAN WITH MATÉ POT.

Dressed in nothing but a very clean gown of white cotton, these dark ladies and gentlemen rush to the station to buy their tickets, sometimes making themselves rather troublesome to the railway servants, by wanting to be off on their journey before the proper time.

A gentleman who was once visiting in their country was very much amused one day by one of the railway officials placing, close to the gates of the office where the tickets were sold, a number of plastering brushes wet with glue and black pitch, so that any one who attempted to climb over the fastened gate could not do so without touching the black, sticky brushes.

The precaution proved most successful, for the black passengers were exceedingly careful about not soiling their white cotton garments, so they patiently waited outside the gates until permission was given them to enter.

GATHERING YERBA MATÉ.

Other tribes also there are ; among them the Lenguas, who were so named by the white men on account of a peculiar chain ornament worn by the tribe, consisting of a semi-circular piece of wood that was passed through a slit in the lower lip, and that gave it the appearance of a hanging tongue.

A similar ornament is worn by the Botocudos, another tribe, of which we have heard previously.

FOURTH CLASS PASSENGERS—PARLIAMENTARY TRAIN IN PARAGUAY.

The little province of Uruguay, south of Paraguay, is the smallest of all the independent states in South America; and though, like Paraguay, it could tell many a tale of war and bloodshed, the picture it presents now is by no means so dark as formerly.

When the Spaniards ruled there the country produced neither wheat, rye, nor barley ; while now corn is raised in such quantities as to keep numbers of steam, wind, and water-mills in constant work. Besides which, tobacco, and the famous yerba-maté, are being grown successfully.

Cotton, plantain, the sugar-cane, besides many fruits and herbs, also thrive in this little country.

There are, perhaps, few sights more beautiful than a sugar plantation about the month of November, when the canes are in full bloom, or in arrow, as they are said to be.

At that time the canes are sometimes eight feet in height, and as they wave about to and fro they present the appearance of an immense sheet of gold, tinged by the sun's rays with a lovely purple.

The stem at first is of a dark green colour, which gradually changes to a bright yellow; then an arrow or silver wand makes its appearance at the end of the cane, and also a number of blue and white flowers, not at all unlike tufts of feathers. It sometimes happens that these beautiful plantations are accidentally set on fire, and then, in the space of a few minutes, the hard work of hundreds of slaves and the hopes of rich men are utterly destroyed.

As soon as the fire is detected the inhabitants sound what is called the alarm shell, the loud whistle of which is heard from the neighbouring hills, and which acts as a summons to bands of negroes to hasten to the rescue. The anxious planters are generally seen driving about. Indeed, the whole picture must be one that to us, who have never seen it, would be difficult to describe.

Monte Video, the chief town of Uruguay, and so called from the cerro or mount close by, is one of the healthiest, cleanest, and handsomest cities in South America. It is built in the form of an amphitheatre, and you may gain some idea of its attractiveness from the accompanying view from the sea. The houses look

VIEW OF MONTE VIDEO.

very pretty, with the sunlight sparkling upon them; most of them are of one storey only, and they have flat roofs.

The language spoken in Monte Video is, of course, Spanish, but there are a number of foreign residents: Italians, Spaniards, Frenchmen, Brazilians, Germans, and Englishmen; indeed, it is said these number no less than 180 out of every 1,000 of the population.

CHAPTER XV.

NOT far from the yerba-maté country lies the land of the great prairies of South America, or the pampas, as they are called.

This country is the Argentine Republic, or La Plata, and, like Chili and Peru, once belonged to Spain, but has since rebelled, and is now a republic in its own right.

The first of modern travellers who found his way to the great river Rio de la Plata was a Spanish mariner of the name of Solis, who died before he had done little more than take a peep into the strange land. The next visitor we hear of is the famous Sebastian Cabot, who was tempted by the sight of the trinkets he saw the Indians wearing to search

diligently for the gold districts, which of course he
concluded could not be far away. Full of hope, he

SEBASTIAN CABOT.

boldly sailed with his men up some of the great
rivers, hoping at last to be crowned with success
such as no one had ever had before, giving the name
M 2

of "the River of Silver" (which is the meaning of Rio de la Plata) to the great river we now know by that name, and into which so many smaller rivers flow. He was interrupted in his scheme, however, by the sight of a vessel, commanded by another of his countrymen, who had left home on the same errand as himself; so what the two voyagers did, instead of making friends with each other, was to quarrel, because (to tell the truth) they were jealous of each other, and the result of the quarrel was that Don Garcia set off home again, leaving the place free for Sebastian to seek for gold the day through, if he chose to do so. Instead of that, Cabot started home too, suspicious of what Garcia might say to his master, the king, about him; but before doing so he founded the first European colony on the river Plata.

After that time other foreigners—Spaniards, Portuguese, and English—kept arriving and settling down to live in the place, until there was quite a large population of mixed people, with no one to govern them. No wonder, therefore, they began to quarrel, not only among themselves, but with other nations. Even the chiefs among them shot each other.

At last, in 1829, one of these chiefs, called Juan Manuel Rosas, was made governor of the provinces; but instead of his making the country better or happier, he made it very much worse in every way, for he was a wicked, cruel man, and very thankful the inhabitants all were when he was at last defeated in battle and driven away.

Since then the country, in spite of various insurrections and disputes, has become orderly and happy.

A considerable portion of La Plata, or the Argentine

VIEW ON THE PAMPAS

Republic, consists of large plains called the pampas, which in reality are the prairies of South America; though sometimes the term is meant to signify any tract of level land, wherever it may happen to be found. These pampas are the homes not only of thousands of animals but also of the Gauchos and the wild Indians, the former of whom are a race of wild Spaniards well known in this district of South America, and who are the peons, or labourers, employed by large owners of horses and cattle.

Their work is all done on horseback; for there are so many horses in America that they run wild, and are not only used as beasts of burden, but are eaten by the inhabitants. The huts of the Gauchos are made of mud thatched with grass; and very often the cradles of the babies are bullocks' skins swung to the roof. Their work is nearly all performed on horseback, and as they boldly scamper across the pampas, holding in their hands the lasso and bolas (ropes with weights attached to either end), with which to catch the different animals they pursue, they appear to be thoroughly happy. As soon as one horse is tired they catch another, and tire that out also. Like most ignorant people, however, they are often very idle; so instead of taking the trouble to cultivate the ground, in

LASSOING A WILD HORSE.

order to be supplied with vegetables for food, they live entirely upon the wild animals they catch.

Some of them are very musical, and are as delighted to sit playing their guitars as their companions are to hurl their lassos.

They generally wear large soft hats, cloaks called *ponchos,* which are pieces of woollen stuff covering the

A GAUCHO.

back, chest, and arms, trousers, known by the name of
chiripa, of a bright showy colour, a leather belt, called
tirador, and large boots adorned with silver spurs.

Bold, wild, cruel men most of them are, and by no
means such as any of us would like to meet alone in a
thick forest.

The vast plain of the pampas may be divided into
three portions. First, the land of tall thistles, which
wither every year, when rich clover springs up in their
place. Then the land of long grass; and this pampas
grass is very different from any that we see in England.
It consists of coarse tufts of hard, dry grass, which
cover the yellow clay like thousands of little islands.
In the distance the spaces between these little tufts
cannot be seen, so that the pampas look like a great
lawn, and in autumn, when the seeds of the grass are
ripe, they look quite white; so that the large plain is like
a great ocean covered with gently rolling silvery waves.
Then lastly there is the land of low trees and shrubs.

Among the animals that frequent the pampas are
the viscachas, animals about the size of squirrels, and
which are as much dreaded as the prairie dogs are in
North America, for the reason that they burrow into the
land so much that it is quite dangerous to travel on the
plains after dark. Horses, mounted by Guachos, very
frequently stumble in the holes made by them.

The armadillo, the hare of the pampas (a kind of
guinea-pig), the beautiful Argentine skunk, rats, mice,
tiger-cats, deer, pole-cats, the ugly river-hog, the puma,
the jaguar, and serpents of all kinds in abundance, dwell
in these wonderful regions.

As to birds, too, there are plenty of them, from the
tiny humming-bird to the large ostrich, so many of

which are to be found in Patagonia. The condor, also, sometimes finds its way to the pampas, though, as a rule, it makes a point of keeping near its much-loved mountains.

Strange tales have been told about this remarkable bird, all of which are not strictly true.

Some old travellers once said that his plumage could not be pierced by a musket ball—an absurd idea, founded, no doubt, on the fact that it is generally a very difficult business to kill him, on account of his plumage, especially on his wings, being so strong and thick.

The natives, therefore, seldom attempt to shoot the condor. They usually catch it by traps or by the lasso, or kill it by stones flung from slings, or with bolas.

When fully grown it measures between four and five feet, from the point of the beak to the end of the tail, and from the tip of one wing to that of the other it measures twelve to fourteen feet.

In one province a curious method of capturing the condor alive is practised.

A fresh cow-hide, with some fragments of flesh adhering to it, is spread out on one of the level heights, and an Indian, provided with ropes, creeps beneath it, whilst some others station themselves in ambush near the spot, ready to assist him.

Presently a condor, attracted by the smell of the flesh, darts down upon the cow-hide, and then the Indian, who is concealed under it, seizes the bird by the legs, and binds them fast in the skin as in a bag.

The captured condor flaps its wings and tries to fly, but is soon secured, and carried in triumph to the nearest village.

Living condors are often sold in the markets of Chili and Peru, where a very fine one may be bought for a dollar and a half, or about six shillings.

To the astonishment of all the birds and animals, a railway runs across the pampas now. They, no doubt, wonder who the bold flying intruder can be who dares to rush screaming across their domain just when he pleases; forgetting, if they do thus wonder, that they themselves are unlike the very first occupants of their home.

Ages ago the sea tossed its silvery spray where the pampas now are, and under the surface have been found carcases of great sloths and armadillos, and other skeletons of old animals that have been buried in its soil, which must have fallen into the river as it flowed through the forests.

Though like their present descendants in form, the creatures were in those days much larger, the most famous of them all, perhaps, being the Megatherium Cuvieri, an immense sloth, from twelve to eighteen feet long, and with bones larger than those of an elephant.

If trees grew in those days this sloth was so huge that it certainly could not have climbed them, as the present sloths do now, back downward.

Instead of attempting that performance, it is thought that it used actually to uproot the whole tree, in order to get the foliage that it wanted for food.

A great many other immense skeletons of animals have been found. So many there are that it is almost impossible to dig deeply in any part of the pampas without finding some such remains.

The principal town of this republic is Buenos Ayres,

VIEW IN BUENOS AYRES.

which, in 1535, was founded by a wealthy speculator, who, on account of its mild, delightful climate, gave it the name of Santa Maria de Buenos Aires, or "Saint Mary of the Good Airs."

It is a sea-port town, but unfortunately has a sloping shore, so that vessels attempting to land can only do so at high tide ; at low tide they are sent back again.

IN THE SUBURBS OF MENDOZA.

Mendoza, another town of great beauty, is built upon some ruins, which were all that were left of a former town after a dreadful earthquake with which it was visited.

As we have heard, South America has been visited many times by these earthquakes, and that at Mendoza, in 1861, must have been very terrible.

One Sunday evening in March, during Lent, when

the churches were full of worshippers, a sudden swelling of the river was observed, then the ground shook, a strange rumbling was heard below, and in a few seconds afterwards thousands of poor creatures were buried alive.

The few people that escaped, scarcely knowing what had happened, ran about amid clouds of dust, mingled with flashes of fire, looking for their homes and their friends; but they had to look in vain—nothing remained but a mass of rubbish and a number of dead or dying human beings.

It sometimes happens before the arrival of an earthquake certain signs are observed as warnings to the inhabitants of what is at hand. Dogs howl, and the other animals appear uneasy, as if they were seeking for some hiding-place from danger. But there were no such warnings at the time of this fearful Mendoza earthquake; within the space of only a few seconds the town was nothing but a mass of ruins.

A Frenchman who was there at the time tells us that as he was walking through the street he felt himself all at once lifted into the air, then thrown many feet away, he did not know where.

The fall made him insensible, but as soon as he recovered consciousness he looked round to see which road he should take to reach his hotel—the only house in the place that he knew, and the kind host of which, also a Frenchman, was his only friend.

The clouds of dust were so great that he had no idea how to proceed, so he remained where he was all night.

The next morning, with great difficulty, he retraced his steps to the hotel, but, on reaching it, all that met

his gaze was a mass of broken beams and crushed stones. The whole family had perished.

A similar fate had been the lot of many others, for it is said that on that dreadful occasion as many as ten or twelve thousand persons were destroyed.

1.—RUINS OF CHURCH OF SAN DOMINGO

2.—RUE ST NICHOLAS, IN MENDOZA.

The present town, so elegantly built and so flourishing, has little left to remind the stranger of its past calamity. It happened so long ago that with many of its inhabitants it is almost forgotten.

Like our joys and sorrows, which, as years roll on, become nothing but memories of the past, so this terrible earthquake of twenty years ago is a thing of the past also, taking its place, of course, among the dark spots in the world's history, where it will ever remain a mystery inexplicable, in the same way that sorrow, and pain, and evil of every kind will always be a mystery to us.

The next country to which, for a short time, we will turn our attention is Patagonia, lying quite to the south of South America. You have, no doubt, heard how tall the inhabitants are who live there, for the Patagonians have long been famous for their great height; though, at the same time, some travellers tell us that many of our countrymen are quite as tall as these Tehuelche Indians, which is another name for the Patagonians.

In the year 1520 a great explorer named Magellan landed on the coast of their country, and he was very much amused at the sight of these huge creatures. They were much bigger than the Spaniards he had left behind, and because they wore shoes made of the skin of the animal called guanaco, his men gave them the name of Patagones, which word means *large feet*.

They paint their bodies, not only for the sake of making themselves look smart, but with the idea of protecting their skin from the cold, and rain, and sun. Those of them who prefer real clothing, make mantles out of guanaco fur, and boots from either the skin of a

VIEW IN MENDOZA

horse or that of a puma.   These garments are made by
the women, who must be very clever workwomen, for the
needles they use are nothing but pieces of bone sharp-
ened to a point, and the thread is made from the sinews
of the guanaco.   We all of us, no doubt, should find the
cloaks they wear very inconvenient, but the Indians,
even on horseback, appear quite comfortable in them.

Like most savages, both the men and women are
very fond of ornaments, such as large square ear-rings,
and necklaces of all descriptions.   A comical appearance
they present, you may be sure.   When seated on their
horses they trot off to the hunt with their painted bodies
decked out in feathers and jewellery.   Their houses, or
toldos, as they are called, are simply tents made by
planting stakes of wood into the ground, and then
covering them with the skins of animals.

Their favourite objects of pursuit are the ostrich and
the guanaco.   The ostrich, we well know, is the huge
swift-footed bird who buries his head in the sand when
he finds there is no escape for him from the hunters, and
is mentioned by one of the oldest poets that ever lived—
the long-suffering Job, who speaks of the ostrich leaving
her eggs in the earth, and warming them in the dust.

The charge long made against the ostrich, however,
for neglecting its young, is partly explained when we
are told that it is only during the day it leaves its eggs,
because then the heat of the sun is sufficient to hatch
them.   During the night it sits upon them, when the
cold would be too great, and, strange to say, it is the
male bird that hatches and looks after the young, being,
as far as is known, the only male bird that does so.

During rainy weather this so-called cruel parent will
sit for six or seven days without leaving the nest, and

without food. In fine weather he may stray away for an hour or two in the evening, but if, during his absence, one egg should be either missing or broken, he on his return becomes so furious that he will dash the remaining eggs to pieces, and dance round the nest as if mad with anger.

A plan of catching ostriches, adopted by some of the wild men, is for one of them, having found a nest, to remove all the eggs and seat himself upon it, and there quietly to await the return of the bird. As soon as it makes its appearance, before it has had time to recover its surprise at finding him there instead of its eggs, he shoots it with a poisoned arrow.

In Africa, when the natives wish to cook an ostrich's egg, they set it upright on a fire, and after making a hole at the top of it, they insert a forked stick, which they stir round and round, until—as they think—the egg is fit for eating. The shell, being, as we know, very thick and strong, is applied to various uses, but principally as a vessel for water.

African girls may be seen coming down to the fountains from their dwellings, each carrying on her back a kaross, or net, containing from twelve to fifteen egg-shells, which have been emptied by a small aperture at one end. These they fill with water, and then close the hole tightly with grass.

The flesh of the ostrich serves excellently for food, and his feathers the Indians sell to people who trade in them.

The guanacos, which are to be seen in great numbers all over Patagonia, are very quick runners too. The head of this animal is like that of a camel; his body is like a deer's, only it is covered with a yellowish kind of wool, and he neighs like a horse. It is in the skin of

N 2

one of these animals, made into what is called a capa by
the Indian women, that the Patagonian ostrich hunters
are arrayed, when, mounted on their horses, they fly
across the pampas after the swift-footed birds. These
capas, made from the skins of the young guanacos, are
extremely warm, and serve well to protect the wearers
of them from the cold winds that blow over the pampas.

PATAGONIAN INDIANS.

The plan adopted for catching these animals is
rather curious, and one which makes a fine day's sport
or the hunters. Around a large open space of ground
number of posts are fixed in the form of a large circle;
a piece of string is then carried from one post to another,

and in the spaces large sheets of paper or linen are hung.
When this is done, the real fun begins. The hunters—
who may be men, women, or even children—scatter
themselves in all directions, and try to chase as many
guanacos as possible from the mountains around towards
the enclosure which has been made.

A large opening is of course made where the animals
can enter; and the
hunters make so
much noise, shout-
ing, screaming, and
throwing their sticks
and weapons about,
that the frightened
creatures before long
are assembled in the
enclosure. There
the poor things
scamper about, and
would like to rush
out again, because
of course they could
easily leap the lines
of cord, but the fly-
ing sheets waving
about in the breeze
so terrify them that

they do not dare to approach them, and thus are very
soon put to death by their pursuers.

Horses abound, too, in the country, and are very
useful to the Patagonians in their hunting excursions.

The weapon chiefly used by these wild hunters is
called the bolas, which in their hands answers all the

purposes of firearms or bows and arrows. It is made by covering two round stones or pieces of lead with leather, and then joining them together with thongs, which very frequently are the sinews from the legs of the ostrich. The Indians swing the bolas quickly round their heads, and then throw them at the animal they are chasing.

Nearly always the balls get twisted round whatever part of the body they fall on, so that the animal cannot run, and thus the hunter gains possession of it.

There is not much to be said about the religion of these people, though it seems that the poor creatures, in spite of their barbarity, have a belief of some kind.

From time to time Christian missionaries have gone and lived among them, and have tried to civilise them, and teach them in many ways, and no doubt the recollection of what these good men have said is still in their minds.

They think that a great good Spirit made all Indians and animals, but that now he takes no notice or care of them; consequently they care little about him in return.

Another bad spirit, whose name is Gualichu, is of far more importance in their estimation, because they think that he is continually contriving mischief for them; so they spare no trouble in trying either to drive him away or to prevent his becoming angry. The medicine-man is one of their number who is supposed to be able to see this evil spirit, and to have influence with him. He has, therefore, plenty to do in the way of magical performances of one kind or another to keep the Gualichu calm and serene.

One very strange custom among these people is that of gathering together all a dead man's possessions and

burning them; consequently there is no such thing in
Patagonia as a child inheriting the father's property,
because, however rich a man may be in horses, dogs,
bolas, clothes, or anything else, all are gathered together
in a heap at his death and burned.

In our country, when dear friends die and leave us,
we have pleasure in thinking about them, and we do all
we can to keep the remembrance of their kind good
deeds fresh in our memory. Instead of that the Patagonians try to forget their dead friends; and they
think that the burning of all this property helps them
to do so, because then there is nothing left to remind
them of the one that has gone.

After this performance—which of course appears to us
useless and extravagant—the body of the man is wrapped
in a coat of mail, if he should have happened to own
one, if not, in guanaco skins; and in the skin with him
are placed his hunting and warlike weapons, and also
any objects of value that he very much cared for when
living; and these, with the body, are fastened securely
upon the dead man's favourite horse.

In order to make the procession still more mournful,
the poor horse has to endure the pain of having one of
its hind legs broken, after which it has to go limping on
under its load until it reaches the last resting-place of
its master.

All the women friends of the Indian widow join in the
procession, and mingle their shrieks and cries of agony
with hers, and the men of the party paint their bodies
black. On reaching the grave—which is usually chosen
on the summit of a high hill—the body is laid in it, after
which the poor lame horse is thrown in also, and very
often with it a number of other animals, which will

be needed, so the Patagonians think, as food by the dead man in the unknown world to which he has travelled. After many days of weeping and lamentation, the widow's friends

A PATAGONIAN FUNERAL. — THE ANIMALS TO BE KILLED.

take her to the house of her parents; and thus ends a Patago-

nian fu-neral.

At the south of Patagonia is a group of islands lying on the other side of the Straits of Magellan, where the inhabitants are more barbarous than even the Patagonians. When Magellan first saw the spot, a number of fires were burn-

A PATAGONIAN FUNERAL.— THE BODY.

ing in different places, so he called it the " Land of Fire."

Most likely the fires were lighted for cooking purposes, as the Fuegians greatly object to eating raw meat of any kind.

Unlike the Patagonians, they are short and stunted, and although there is plenty of snow and hail and frost, both the women and men wear scarcely any clothing. They paint their bodies certainly, and deck themselves with finery. One favourite ornament they wear is a necklace made of the teeth of some fish ; but they have become so accustomed to being without clothing that they feel no want of it. Perhaps nowhere were found human beings so closely resembling dumb animals as these Fuegians.

In late years, however, many of them have been persuaded by missionaries to change their brutal savage mode of life for one of industry and civilisation. It is therefore quite possible that in course of time the rest of them may be induced to do so also; and perhaps even in the wild region of Tierra del Fuego there may be homes as peaceful and refined as those in happy England.

CHAPTER XVI.

CONCLUSION.

AND now, after making this short acquaintance with a few of our South American friends, we must for the present say farewell to them, hoping to meet with them again in the same way on some future occasion.

If the opportunity were given us of shaking hands with any of them, we should surely, every one, do so as willingly with the black man as with the white one, and not recoil from touching him on account of his dark skin or coarse features.

The tiger, as we are told, for some unknown reason, prefers the negro's flesh as food to that of the white man. With us, although it is hardly likely that we should ever really prefer a black man to a white one, we know very well that under that dark, swarthy skin of his, beats a heart as tender as our own, and that he is as capable of loving as we are.

It may be that the wild savage life he has always
led has hardened his nature, and made him almost as
fit a companion for the animals he hunts as for refined
educated human beings ; and as to purity, and gentle-
ness, and goodness, with the meaning that is conveyed
to our minds by the very sound of the words, he simply
knows nothing about them, because no one has ever
explained to him their hidden beauty.

Still, when we bear in mind that, dwellers in whatever country we may be in—cold, icy regions, or in
warm, sunny lands, in the new world or the old, in
past ages or at the present time—we are all children
of one great family, and that within every one of us
is a spark of that Divine nature which we inherit from
our heavenly Father, we cannot but hope that some
day, however far in the future it may be, there will be
no more cruelty and wrong, but that we shall all alike
be ruled by love.

In the endeavour to bring about such a happy con-
dition, it is in the power of every one of us to give a
helping hand, by beginning from this very hour to
crush in ourselves all that is mean, and selfish, and
trivial, and to lead pure, generous, noble lives.

Let us all try to remember how much greater our
advantages have been than those of hundreds of our
fellow-creatures.   By doing so we shall banish from our
minds anything like a proud or boastful spirit, and we
shall, no doubt, instead feel ashamed that we have made
so little use of our advantages.

After that, let us all try to forget ourselves and
even our shortcomings too, and look around to see in
which way we can best lessen pain and sorrow, or how
we can prevail upon travellers who are running in the

broad road that leads to destruction to turn aside into the strait and narrow way that leads to life.

To find work of this kind we need not look very long, neither is it necessary to travel into foreign lands in search of it. There is plenty of work for us, every one of us, close at our feet; the difficulty will be how to accomplish all we wish.

One duty among others, that we who stay at home need not neglect, will be to help those who leave their native land and their homes to risk their lives among uncivilised people, such as we have lately been hearing about; but, of course, in order to do that we need not neglect our own work, and if any of us feel inclined to be discouraged, let us think of the truth conveyed in the following lines :—

> " Though we see, on looking round us,
>   Man to wickedness is prone,
> Though the snares of vice surround us,
>   Virtue's paths but rarely known,
> Well we know that in our nature
>   Is a spark of life divine ;
> We must free the soul from thraldom,
>   If we wish that spark to shine.
> We must all be up and stirring
>   With determination true ;
> Young and old men, rich and poor men
>   All have got their work to do.

> " Life is but a scene of labour,
>   Each one has his task assigned ;
> We must all assist our neighbour,
>   When we see him lag behind.
> We must strive by education
>   Man's condition to improve,

And bind men of every station
  In a bond of mutual love.
All must then be up and stirring
  With determination true;
Young men, old men, rich men, poor men,
  Ye all have your work to do."

THE END.

CASSELL, PETTER, GALPIN & CO., BELLE SAUVAGE WORKS, LONDON, E.C.

"HEART CHORDS"

A Series of Little Books calculated to Stimulate, Guide, and Strengthen the Christian Life.

Arrangements have been made with the following Eminent Divines to contribute to the Series:—The Right Rev. Bishop COTTERILL, the Very Rev. Dean MONTGOMERY, the Very Rev. Dean BICKERSTETH, the Very Rev. Dean EDWARDS, the Very Rev. Dean BOYLE, the Rev. Canon FARRAR, the Rev. Canon BOYD CARPENTER, the Rev. Prof. BLAIKIE, the Rev. Prebendary CHADWICK, the Rev. P. B. POWER, the Rev. Dr. MATHESON, and the Rev. E. E. JENKINS.

The Volumes are produced in the best style, neatly and appropriately bound in cloth, red edges, and published at

ONE SHILLING EACH.

LIST OF VOLUMES.

MY WORK FOR GOD.
By the Right Rev. Bishop COTTERILL.

MY OBJECT IN LIFE.
By the Rev. CANON FARRAR, D.D.

MY BIBLE.
By the Rev. Canon BOYD CARPENTER.

MY SOUL.
By the Rev. P. B. POWER, M.A.

MY HEREAFTER.
By the Very Rev. Dean BICKERSTETH.

(Continued over.)

MY FATHER'S HOUSE.
By the Very Rev. Dean EDWARDS.

MY WALK WITH GOD.
By the Very Rev. Dean MONTGOMERY.

MY ASPIRATIONS.
By the Rev. GEO. MATHESON, D.D., of Innellan, and Baird Lecturer.

MY BODY.
By the Rev. Prof. W. G. BLAIKIE, D.D., Prof. in New College, Edinburgh.

MY AIDS TO THE DIVINE LIFE.
By the Very Rev. Dean BOYLE.

MY EMOTIONAL LIFE.
By the Rev. Preb. CHADWICK, D.D.

The Series will also contain a Work by the Rev. E. F. JENKINS, M.A., Secretary of the Wesleyan Missionary Society, and Ex-President of the Conference.

Each of the above Volumes will contain about 128 pages, divided into brief chapters, easily read by busy people, suitable for perusal at Morning and Evening Devotion, in the Family Circle, in the School, Bible Class, and on the Sabbath Day.

It is intended that this Series may minister to all that is true and strong in moral character.

CASSELL, PETTER, GALPIN & CO., *Ludgate Hill, London.*

An Illustrated

CATALOGUE

OF BOOKS

Suitable for Young People

And the Little Ones.

PUBLISHED BY

CASSELL & COMPANY, LIMITED,

LUDGATE HILL, LONDON.

Little Folks. The MAGAZINE for all GIRLS & BOYS.
Monthly, 6d.

"Every one ought to know by this time that LITTLE FOLKS is the best magazine for children."—*Graphic.*

"If any father of a family—of ages ranging from eight to fifteen years—knows how to spend sixpence a month in literature to better

(From *Little Folks.*)

purpose than in the purchase of LITTLE FOLKS, we should be glad if he would enlighten us."—*Literary World.*

The NEW VOLUME *of LITTLE FOLKS contains nearly* **500** **Illustrations,** *and forms one of the most charming Gift-Books for Children of all ages. Price* **3s. 6d.**; *or cloth gilt, gilt edges,* **5s.**

Cassell & Company, Limited, Ludgate Hill, London.

A TREASURY FOR THE LITTLE ONES.

Bo-Peep (Yearly Volume). Illustrated throughout with Original Pictures drawn by LIZZIE LAWSON, ERNEST GRISET, E. J. WALKER, and other Artists. Elegant Picture Boards, 2s. 6d. ; or cloth, gilt edges, 3s. 6d. *** *Also published* MONTHLY, *price* ..

(From *Bo-Peep.*)

* The beautiful Original Illustrations, the luxurious paper, the bold type, the care given to every detail of production, has placed BO-PEEP at the head of books for the very little ones. Beautiful Illustrations by the first Artists literally load its pages, and the denizens of the nursery are themselves led on to read about them by the clearness of the type and the simplicity of the stories and verses.

Cassell & Company, Limited, Ludgate Hill, London.

Brave Lives and Noble. By C. L. MATÉAUX. Illustrated. Crown 4to, gilt edges, 7s. 6d.

WINSTANLEY'S LIGHTHOUSE.

. In this volume the popular authoress of " Home Chat " and numerous other works which have obtained an immense sale in England and abroad, relates after her own well-known manner the lives of brave and noble men and women who have illuminated the pages of history. The narrative is illustrated throughout with an abundance of bold and striking Illustrations, and makes a handsome Gift Book.

Living Pages from Many Ages. With upwards of 50 full-page Illustrations. Cloth gilt, 5s.

" A capital prize."—*Sunday School Chronicle.*

Cassell & Company, Limited, Ludgate Hill, London.

Myself and My Friends. By OLIVE PATCH.

With numerous Illustrations. Crown 4to, cloth, gilt edges, 5s.

(From *Myself and My Friends.*)

*. This charming Volume for children is uniform with "A PARCEL OF CHILDREN," "FAMILIAR FRIENDS," and other popular works by the same Authoress. MYSELF AND MY FRIENDS gives delightful reading for young people, and is illustrated on nearly every page with beautiful and interesting pictures.

Cassell & Company, Limited, Ludgate Hill, London.

Daisy Dimple's Scrap Book. A Book of Picture Stories. Royal 4to, size 12½ in. by 10 in. 192 pages. In handsome Illuminated Wrapper Boards, 5s.; cloth gilt, gilt edges, 7s. 6d.

OUT FOR A WALK.   AN INTRODUCTION.

(From *Daisy Dimple's Scrap Book.*)

** This large Scrap Book, containing nearly One Thousand entertaining Pictures, will prove a never-failing source of attraction to the little ones.

The Mother Goose Goslings. By ELEANOR W. TALBOT. With Coloured Pictures. 4to, 3s. 6d.

** This is a book of favourite Nursery Rhymes, with Coloured Pictures by an American Artist on every page. These pictures are not only extremely pretty and picturesque, but will be of especial interest as showing the English people the American ideas of "Art for the Nursery."

Cassell & Company, Limited, Ludgate Hill, London.

The Quiver. Illustrated Magazine for Sunday Reading. Monthly, 6d.

"A safer and more interesting magazine we do not know than THE QUIVER."— *Standard.*

(From *The Quiver.*)

The YEARLY VOLUME of THE QUIVER, price 7s. 6d., contains about 250 Original Stories and Papers and 150 Illustrations, and forms a veritable library in itself.

Cassell's Family Magazine. Yearly Volume, 9s.; Monthly, 7d.

"CASSELL'S FAMILY MAGAZINE has long established its well-deserved reputation as THE FAVOURITE MAGAZINE."—*Morning Post.*

"Most assuredly the Magazine for the Household."— *Civil Service Gazette.*

Cassell & Company, Limited, Ludgate Hill, London.

LIBRARY FOR FAMILY READING.
All Illustrated and bound in cloth gilt.   3s. 6d. each.

(From *My Guardian.*)

My Guardian. By Ada Cambridge. With numerous Illustrations by Frank Dicksee, A.R.A. 3s. 6d.

School Girls. By the late Annie Carey. 3s. 6d.

Deepdale Vicarage. 3s. 6d.

In Duty Bound. 3s 6d.

The Half Sisters. 3s. 6d.

Peggy Oglivie's Inheritance. By I. Craig-Knox. 3s. 6d.

The Family Honour. By Mrs. C. L. Balfour. 3s. 6d.

Esther West. By Isa Craig-Knox. 3s. 6d.

Working to Win. By Maggie Symington. 3s. 6d.

THREE-AND-SIXPENNY LIBRARY.

Jane Austen and Her Works. By Sarah Tytler. With Steel Portrait. Cloth gilt, 3s. 6d.

Mission Life in Greece and Palestine. By Mrs. E. R. Pitman. Illustrated. Cloth, gilt edges, 3s. 6d.

Heroines of the Mission Field. By Mrs. E. R. Pitman. Illustrated. Cloth, gilt edges, 3s. 6d.

Better than Good. A Story for Girls. By Annie E. Ridley. With full-page Illustrations. Cloth, gilt edges, 3s. 6d.

The Dingy House at Kensington. With Four full-page Illustrations. Crown 8vo, cloth, gilt edges, 3s. 6d.

The above Five Volumes can also be had bound in morocco, cloth sides, full gilt, price 6s. each.

Cassell & Company, Limited, Ludgate Hill, London.

The Child's Life of Christ. Complete in one handsome volume. Illustrated throughout with Original Illustrations, executed expressly for the work by the first artists. Demy 4to, cloth, gilt edges, 21s.

AN EASTERN CARAVAN. (From *The Child's Life of Christ.*)

UNIFORM WITH THE "CHILD'S LIFE OF CHRIST."

The Child's Bible. With 200 Original Illustrations. 125th Thousand. Demy 4to, 830 pp. Cloth, gilt edges, £1 1s. *Cheap Edition,* 7s. 6d.

Day-Dawn in Dark Places; or Wanderings and Work in Bechwanaland, South Africa. By the Rev. JOHN MACKENZIE, Tutor of Mizput Institution, Kuruman. Illustrated throughout. Cloth, 3s. 6d.

. This is a book of African travel and of African life. It is full of stirring incident and adventure. The Author is often among wild beasts, and always more or less among wild men. The ethnologist, and those who have followed the course of our political relations with South Africa, will find something to interest them in the original information here given concerning the Bushmen and other tribes of the interior. In his account of Mission work, the Author tells of great sufferings heroically endured—of death calmly met.

Cassell & Company, Limited, Ludgate Hill, London.

Leslie's Songs for Little Folks. Containing 18
Pieces of Children's Music by HENRY LESLIE, and a
New and Original Drawing by J. E. MILLAIS, R.A., as
Frontispiece, together with Six other Illustrations by
the same Artist.   Small 4to, cloth, 1s. 6d.

(From *Leslie's Songs for Little Folks.*)

** This is a Cheap Edition in One Volume of the very popular works, "Little
Songs for me to Sing," and "Leslie's Songs for Little Folks," originally published
at 5s. and 3s. 6d. each respectively.   At the price it is now issued it is calculated to
find its way into thousands of homes where pretty, simple melodies for children are
desired.

Cassell & Company, Limited, Ludgate Hill, London.

A Moonbeam Tangle. Original Fairy Tales. By SIDNEY SHADBOLT. With numerous Illustrations. Cloth, 3s. 6d.

Elfie under the Sea, and other Stories. By E. L. P. With Full-page Illustrations. Crown 4to, paper boards, price 3s. 6d.

The Favorite Album of Fun and Fancy. Illustrated. Crown 4to, 3s. 6d.

(From *Little Hinges*.)

Stories of Girlhood; or, the Brook and the River. By SARAH DOUDNEY. Cloth, gilt edges, 5s.

Truth Will Out. By JEANIE HERING. Cloth, 3s. 6d.

Little Hinges. By M. BONAVIA HUNT. Illustrated by M. ELLEN EDWARDS. Cloth gilt, 2s. 6d.

Cassell & Company, Limited, Ludgate Hill, London.

CASSELL'S HALF-CROWN STORY BOOKS.

By Popular Authors, handsomely illustrated throughout. Cloth, gilt, 2s. 6d. each.

Pen's Perplexities. By M. B. HUNT. Illustrated. 2s. 6d.

Margaret's Enemy.   By the Author of "Little Hinges." &c.   Illustrated.   2s. 6d.

(From *Pen's Perplexities.*)

Little Empress Joan. By M. B. HUNT. Illustrated. 2s. 6d.

Golden Days. By JEANIE HERING. New Edition. 2s. 6d.

Notable Shipwrecks. By UNCLE HARDY. 2s. 6d.

The Wonders of Common Things. 2s. 6d.

Cassell & Company, Limited, Ludgate Hill, London.

HANDSOME GIFT-BOOKS FOR LITTLE PEOPLE.

Old Proverbs with New Pictures. With 64 Fac-
simile Coloured Plates from Original Designs by LIZZIE
LAWSON. The Text by C. L. MATÉAUX. Crown 4to, 6s.

"My Diary." With 12 Coloured Plates and 366 small
Woodcuts, together with blank spaces for every day in
the year. Boards, 1s.; roan, 2s.

(From *The Old Fairy Tales.*)

Little Folks' Picture Album. Containing 168 large
Pictures. Cloth, gilt edges, 5s.

Little Folks' Picture Gallery. Containing nearly
150 Pictures, with Simple Rhymes. Cloth gilt, 5s.

The Old Fairy Tales. With numerous Original Illustrations. Boards, 1s.; cloth gilt, 1s. 6d.

Three Wise Old Couples. A Ludicrous Book of
Laughable Rhymes. With 16 Coloured Plates. 5s.

The " Little Folks" Album of Music. Illustrated.
Crown 4to, cloth, gilt edges, 3s. 6d.

Cassell & Company, Limited, Ludgate Hill, London.

Cassell's Two-Shilling Story Books. All Illustrated throughout, and containing Stories for Young People. Crown 8vo, handsomely bound in cloth gilt, 2s. each.

(From *In Mischief Again*.)

Cassell & Company, Limited, Ludgate Hill, London.

CASSELL'S EIGHTEENPENNY STORY BOOKS.

All Illustrated, and containing Stories for Young People.
1s. 6d. each.

(From *Three Wee Ulster Lasses.*)

Cassell & Company, Limited, Ludgate Hill, London.

Cassell's Shilling Story Books. All Illustrated, and containing Interesting Stories for Young People. Extra fcap. 8vo, cloth gilt, 1s. each.

(From *Thorns and Tangles.*)

Thorns and Tangles. The Story
  of Bertie Grafton's Troubles.
The Cuckoo in the Robin's Nest.
Surly Bob.
The Giant's Cradle.
Shag and Doll; and Other
  Stories.
Aunt Lucia's Locket; and Other
  Stories.
Among the Redskins.
The Ferryman of Brill.
Harry Maxwell; and Other
  Stories.

The Magic Mirror.
The Cost of Revenge.
Clever Frank.
A Banished Monarch.
John's Mistake.
Pearl's Fairy Flower.
The History of Five Little Pit-
  chers who had very Large Ears.
Diamonds in the Sand; and
  Other Stories.

Cassell & Company, Limited, Ludgate Hill, London.

CASSELL'S SIXPENNY STORY BOOKS.

All Illustrated, and containing interesting Stories by well-known writers. Bound in attractive coloured boards, price 6d. each.

The Elchester College Boys. By Mrs. HENRY WOOD. And other Stories.

The Boat Club. By OLIVER OPTIC. And other Stories.

Helpful Nelly; and Other Stories.

(From *My First Cruise.*)

The Delft Jug. By SILVERPEN. And other Stories.

My First Cruise. By W. H. G. KINGSTON.

Lottie's White Frock; and other Stories.

Only Just Once; and other Stories.

The Little Peacemaker. By MARY HOWITT.

Cassell & Company, Limited, Ludgate Hill, London.

GIFT BOOKS FOR BOYS.

Heroes of Britain in Peace and War.   VOL. I.
Popular Edition, with about 150 Illustrations.   Cloth, 5s.

THE DEFENDERS OF ROKKE'S DRIFT.   (From *Heroes of Britain.*)

Modern Explorers.   By THOMAS FROST.   Profusely
Illustrated.   Crown 4to, 176 pages, cloth, gilt edges, 5s.

Half-Hours with the Early Explorers.   By T.
FROST.   Illustrated.   Fcap. 4to, cloth, gilt edges, 5s.

Cassell & Company, Limited, Ludgate Hill, London.

THE BOYS' LIBRARY.

Handsomely bound in cloth, gilt edges.

The Story of Captain Cook. Illustrated. 3s. 6d.

At the South Pole. By W. H. G. KINGSTON. 3s. 6d.

(From *The Three Homes*.)

The Three Homes. By F. T. L. HOPE. 3s. 6d.

The Romance of Trade. Illustrated. 3s. 6d.

Soldier and Patriot. The Story of George Washington. By F. M. OWEN. With Map and Illustrations. 3s. 6d.

Pictures of School Life and Boyhood. Selected from the best Authors by P. FITZGERALD, M.A. 2s. 6d.

The Young Man in the Battle of Life. By the Rev. Dr. LANDELS. 2s. 6d.

Cassell & Company, Limited, Ludgate Hill, London.

STANDARD BOOKS FOR BOYS.

Wild Animals and Birds ; their Haunts and Habits. By Dr. ANDREW WILSON. Illustrated. Demy 4to, cloth, 7s. 6d.

Wild Adventures in Wild Places. By Dr. GORDON STABLES, R.N. Illustrated throughout. Cloth gilt, 5s.

A Cruise in Chinese Waters. By Capt. A. F. LINDLEY. With 50 Engravings. Cloth gilt, 5s.

Decisive Events in History. With 16 full-page Original Illustrations. *Fifth Edition.* Boards, 3s. 6d. ; cloth gilt, 5s.

(From *Wild Adventures in Wild Places.*)

Cassell's Swiss Family Robinson. Illustrated. Cloth, 3s. 6d.

Cassell's Robinson Crusoe. Illustrated. Cloth, 3s. 6d.

Jungle, Peak, and Plain. By Dr. GORDON STABLES, R.N. Illustrated. Cloth gilt, 5s.

Cassell & Company, Limited, Ludgate Hill, London.

POPULAR BOOKS FOR YOUNG PEOPLE,
Fully Illustrated.

Bound in coloured boards, 3s. 6d. each ; or
cloth, gilt edges, 5s. each.

. *Nearly* **200,000** *Copies of the following Works have
already been sold :—*

Home Chat with our Young Folks.
By C. L. MATÉAUX.
" Never was instruction more admirably given than in this
attractive volume."—*British Quarterly.*

Peeps Abroad for Folks at Home.
By C. L. MATÉAUX.
" Pleasantly written. Children will read it with interest."—
Guardian.

Sunday Chats with our Young Folks.
By C. L. MATÉAUX.
" A delightful book either for Sundays or week-days ; the
illustrations alone would be a treat to children."—*Athenæum.*

Around and About Old England.
By C. L. MATÉAUX.
" The volume is a handsome one, and will be prized by boys
and girls alike."—*Standard.*

Stories about Animals.   By Rev. T.
JACKSON, M.A.
" Full of excellent pictures and a vast number of interesting
stories, it will be the favourite of the nursery."—*Echo.*

Stories about Birds.   By M. and E.
KIRBY.
" The stories are well told, and the text is illustrated by a
series of excellent engravings."—*Scotsman.*

Paws and Claws.   Being True Stories
of Clever Creatures, Tame and Wild.
" Profusely and charmingly illustrated. A delightful gift-
book."—*Morning Post.*

Field Friends and Forest Foes.
Extra fcap. 4to, cloth gilt, gilt edges, 5s.
" It is a handsome volume as regards both paper and type."—
Athenæum.

Cassell & Company, Limited, Ludgate Hill, London.

THE WORLD IN PICTURES.

The following six volumes are especially suitable for gift-books and Sunday-school prizes, presenting as they do vividly, though incidentally, *pictures of Missionary Enterprise throughout the World.* They are all brightly written, handsomely illustrated, and elegantly bound in cloth gilt, gilt edges :—

The Eastern Wonderland. By D. C. ANGUS. Illustrated. Cloth, gilt edges, 2s. 6d.

THE STREET OF APOTHECARIES, CANTON.
(From *Peeps into China.*)

Peeps into China; or, The Missionary's Children. By E. C. PHILLIPS. With numerous Illustrations. 2s. 6d.

Glimpses of South America. Illustrated. 2s. 6d.

Round Africa. Illustrated. 2s. 6d.

The Land of Temples. Illustrated. 2s. 6d.

The Isles of the Pacific. Illustrated. 2s. 6d.

Cassell & Company, Limited, Ludgate Hill, London.

THE LIBRARY OF WONDERS.

A Series of Gift Books for Boys. All Illustrated throughout with striking Engravings. Crown 8vo, cloth, gilt edges, 2s. 6d. each.

Wonderful Adventures. A Series of Narratives of Personal Experiences among the Native Tribes of America. 2s. 6d.

Wonders of Animal Instinct. With Illustrative Anecdotes. 2s. 6d.

(From *Wonderful Adventures*.)

Wonderful Balloon Ascents. A History of Balloons and Balloon Voyages. 2s. 6d.

Wonderful Escapes. 2s. 6d.

Wonders of Bodily Strength and Skill in all Ages and in all Countries. 2s. 6d.

Wonders of Water. Revised by R. S. BALL, LL.D. 2s. 6d.

Wonders of Acoustics. 2s. 6d.

Wonders of Architecture. 2s. 6d.

Cassell & Company, Limited, Ludgate Hill, London.

BEAUTIFUL BOOKS FOR YOUNG PEOPLE.

The Wonderland of Work. By C. L. MATÉAUX, Author of "Home Chat." With numerous Original Illustrations. Extra crown 4to, cloth gilt, 320 pages, 7s. 6d.

"A collection of the curiosities of industry, surpassing in its romance the wonders of fairyland."—*British Quarterly Review.*

(From *Tim Trumble's "Little Mother."*)

Tim Trumble's "Little Mother." A Story for Young Folks. By C. L. MATÉAUX. With 18 Illustrations by GIACOMELLI. Extra fcap. 4to, cloth, gilt edges, 5s.

"The book is a charming one, and the illustrations of birds are as good as anything of the kind that we have seen."—*Standard.*

Tiny Houses and their Builders. By the Author of "Poems written for a Child." Illustrated. Cloth gilt, 5s.

"Brimming over with loving observation of the habits and peculiar little ways of these creatures."—*Standard.*

Little Folks' History of England. Cheap Edition. Illustrated throughout. 1s. 6d.

Cassell & Company, Limited, Ludgate Hill, London.

BOOKS FOR LITTLE PEOPLE.

Cassell's Children's Album. Containing nearly 200 Engravings, with Short Stories by UNCLE JOHN. Also several Pieces of Music. Cloth, gilt edges, 3s. 6d.

" Exactly meets a want. A capital book."—*Athenæum.*

Cassell's Children's Sunday Album. With upwards of 150 Engravings, with Simple Stories. 3s. 6d.

(From *Cassell's Children's Album.*)

The Story of Robin Hood. With Plates printed in Colours. Cloth gilt, 2s. 6d.

" A gay little volume, bright with coloured prints."—*Guardian.*

Off to Sea. By W. H. G. KINGSTON. With Illustrations printed in Colours. Cloth gilt, 2s. 6d.

" A very capital book for boys."—*John Bull.*

Books in Words of One Syllable. With Eight Coloured Illustrations in each Volume. Cloth lettered, 2s. 6d. each.

ÆSOP'S FABLES.	THE PILGRIM'S PROGRESS.
SANDFORD AND MERTON.	REYNARD THE FOX.

Cassell & Company, Limited, Ludgate Hill, London.

PICTURE TEACHING BOOKS.

All beautifully illustrated throughout, handsomely
bound, 2s. 6d. each.

Through Picture-Land. By C. L. MATÉAUX. 2s. 6d.
Picture Teaching for Young and Old. 2s. 6d.
Picture Natural History. 2s. 6d.
Scraps of Knowledge for the Little Ones. 2s. 6d.
Great Lessons from Little Things. 2s. 6d.

(From *Picture Teaching for Young and Old.*)

The Children of Holy Scripture. By L. MASSEY.
The Boy Joiner and Model Maker. 2s. 6d.
Pussy Tip-toes' Family. 2s. 6d.
Frisk and His Flock. 2s. 6d.

Cassell & Company, Limited, Ludgate Hill, London.

THE COSY CORNER SERIES.

Story Books for Children, each containing nearly 100 full
page Pictures. Cloth gilt, gilt edges, 2s. each.

SEE-SAW STORIES.
LITTLE CHIMES FOR ALL TIMES.
BRIGHT SUNDAYS.
WEE WILLIE WINKIE.
PET'S POSY OF PICTURES AND
STORIES.
LITTLE TALKS WITH LITTLE
PEOPLE.

STORY FLOWERS FOR RAINY HOURS.
DOT'S STORY BOOK.
BRIGHT RAYS FOR DULL DAYS.
CHATS FOR SMALL CHAT-
TERERS.
PICTURES FOR HAPPY HOURS.
UPS AND DOWNS OF A DONKEY'S
LIFE.

(From *Pet's Posy of Pictures and Stories.*)

The COSY CORNER Books form a favourite Series of Presentation Volumes for Young People, the stories being bright and
attractive, and the pictures full of life and interest.

Cassell & Company, Limited, Ludgate Hill, London.

CASSELL'S CHILDREN'S TREASURIES.

Illustrated throughout.   Cloth, 1s. each.

COCK ROBIN, AND OTHER NURSERY
RHYMES.
THE QUEEN OF HEARTS.
OLD MOTHER HUBBARD.
SIMPLE RHYMES FOR HAPPY TIMES.
TUNEFUL LAYS FOR MERRY DAYS.
CHEERFUL SONGS FOR YOUNG FOLKS.
PRETTY POEMS FOR LITTLE PEOPLE.

THE CHILDREN'S JOY.
OUR PICTURE BOOK.
PRETTY PICTURES AND PLEASANT
STORIES.
TALES FOR THE LITTLE ONES.
MY SUNDAY BOOK OF PICTURES.
SUNDAY GARLAND OF PICTURES AND
STORIES.

SUNDAY READINGS FOR LITTLE FOLKS.

THE SCHOOL BAND.   (*From Our Picture Book.*)

CASSELL'S CHILDREN'S TREASURIES form a beautifully Illustrated Series of Gift-Books for the Young, printed in large type, and written in simple and interesting language.

Cassell & Company, Limited, Ludgate Hill, London.

RECREATION FOR THE CHILDREN.

"LITTLE FOLKS" SERIES, to Teach Young People how to Draw and Paint. Price 1s. each, or handsomely bound in cloth gilt, 2s. each.

FORTY-FIFTH THOUSAND.

Pictures to Paint. With numerous Original Coloured Plates. With accompanying Outline Engravings.

TWENTY-FIFTH THOUSAND.

The "Little Folks" Illuminating Book. Containing a Series of Texts in Outline, with Coloured Copies for guidance.

Pictures to Paint and Texts to Illuminate. The two above books handsomely bound in cloth, price 2s. 6d.

ONE HUNDRED AND TENTH THOUSAND.

The "Little Folks" Painting Book. A Series of Outline Drawings by KATE GREENAWAY. With amusing Letterpress Descriptive of the Pictures.

THIRTIETH THOUSAND.

The "Little Folks" Nature Painting Book. With numerous Illustrations of well-known British Flowers, Butterflies, Birds, and Animals. Price 1s.

Another "Little Folks" Painting Book. With numerous Illustrations. Handsomely bound in cloth gilt, 2s.

CASSELL & COMPANY, Limited, *Ludgate Hill, London.*

SERIAL PUBLICATIONS.

The Magazine of Art. ENLARGED. Monthly, 1s.

Bible, **Cassell's Illustrated.** Monthly, 7d.

Bible Educator, Cassell's. Monthly, 7d.

Canaries and **Cage Birds.** Monthly, 6d.

Cities *of the World.* Monthly, 7d.

Cookery, Cassell's *Dictionary of.* Monthly, 6d.

Cyclopædia, **Cassell's Concise.** Monthly, 6d.

Dairy Farming. Monthly, 1s.

Dog, The Illustrated **Book of the.** Monthly, 1s.

Doré Bible. Monthly, 7d.

Doré Dante, The. Monthly, 7d.

Doré Gallery, The. Monthly, 7d.

England, **Cassell's History of.** Monthly, 7d. and 8½d.

English Literature, **The Library of.** Monthly, 6d.

Ferns, **European.** Monthly, 7d.

Fisheries **of** *the World.* Monthly, 7d.

Franco-German War, Cassell's History **of** *the.* Monthly, 7d.

Garden Flowers, Familiar. Monthly, 6d.

Greater *London, Cassell's.* Monthly, 7d.

Heroes of Britain in **Peace and War.** Monthly, 6d.

London, *Old and New, Cassell's.* Monthly, 7d.

Cassell & Company, Limited, Ludgate Hill, London.

SERIAL PUBLICATIONS (continued).

Mechanics, Practical Dictionary of. Monthly, 7d.

Music, The History of. Monthly, 7d.

New Testament Commentary for English Readers. Monthly, 7d.

Our Homes, and How to Make them Healthy. Monthly, 7d.

Paxton's Flower Garden. Monthly, 1s.

Peoples of the World, The. Monthly, 7d.

Picturesque America. Monthly, 2s. 6d.

Picturesque Europe. Monthly, 1s.

Popular Educator, Cassell's. Monthly, 6d.

Protestantism. The History of. Monthly, 7d.

Roberts's Holy Land. Monthly, 7d.

Science for All. Monthly, 7d.

Sea: its Stirring Story of Adventure, Peril, and Heroism. The. Monthly, 7d.

Shakspere, The Royal. Monthly, 7d.

St. Paul, The Life and Work of. Monthly, 7d.

Universal History, Cassell's Illustrated. Monthly, 7d.

Wild Birds, Familiar. Monthly, 6d.

Wild Flowers, Familiar. Monthly, 6d.

World of Wonders, The. Monthly, 6d.

*** *Prospectuses of any of the above sent post free on application.*

Cassell & Company, Limited, Ludgate Hill, London.

A List of Catalogues

OF

CASSELL & COMPANY'S PUBLICATIONS,

WHICH WILL BE SENT POST FREE ON APPLICATION.

COMPLETE CATALOGUE.

CASSELL & COMPANY'S COMPLETE CATALOGUE contains particulars of Several Hundred Volumes, including Bibles and Religious Works, Illustrated and Fine-Art Volumes, Children's Books, Dictionaries, Educational Works, History, Natural History, Household and Domestic Treatises, Science, Travels, &c., together with a Synopsis of their numerous Illustrated Serial Publications.

CLASSIFIED CATALOGUE.

A CLASSIFIED CATALOGUE of CASSELL & COMPANY'S Publications, in which their Works are arranged, according to price, from SIXPENCE to TWENTY-FIVE GUINEAS. This will be most convenient to those who may be selecting Volumes for General Reading, Educational Purposes, or Presentation, as it contains particulars of Several Hundred Books so arranged as to show at a glance to an intending purchaser what he can procure with the money he is prepared to expend.

EDUCATIONAL CATALOGUE.

CASSELL & COMPANY'S EDUCATIONAL CATALOGUE contains particulars of their Educational Works and Students' Manuals, including French, German, Latin, History, Grammar, Geography, Spelling, Reading, Writing, Drawing, Euclid, Algebra, Dictionaries, Technical Manuals, &c.

PRIZE BOOKS CATALOGUE.

A CATALOGUE OF SELECTED VOLUMES suitable for School Prizes, Rewards and Presentation, School Libraries, &c.

Cassell & Company, Limited, Ludgate Hill, London.

ILLUSTRATED CATALOGUE.

N.B.—CASSELL'S NEW ILLUSTRATED CATALOGUE, price 2s. 6d., royal 4to size, contains numerous choice Wood Engravings, selected from CASSELL & COMPANY'S Publications, beautifully printed on fine paper.

Cassell & Company, Limited, Ludgate Hill, London.